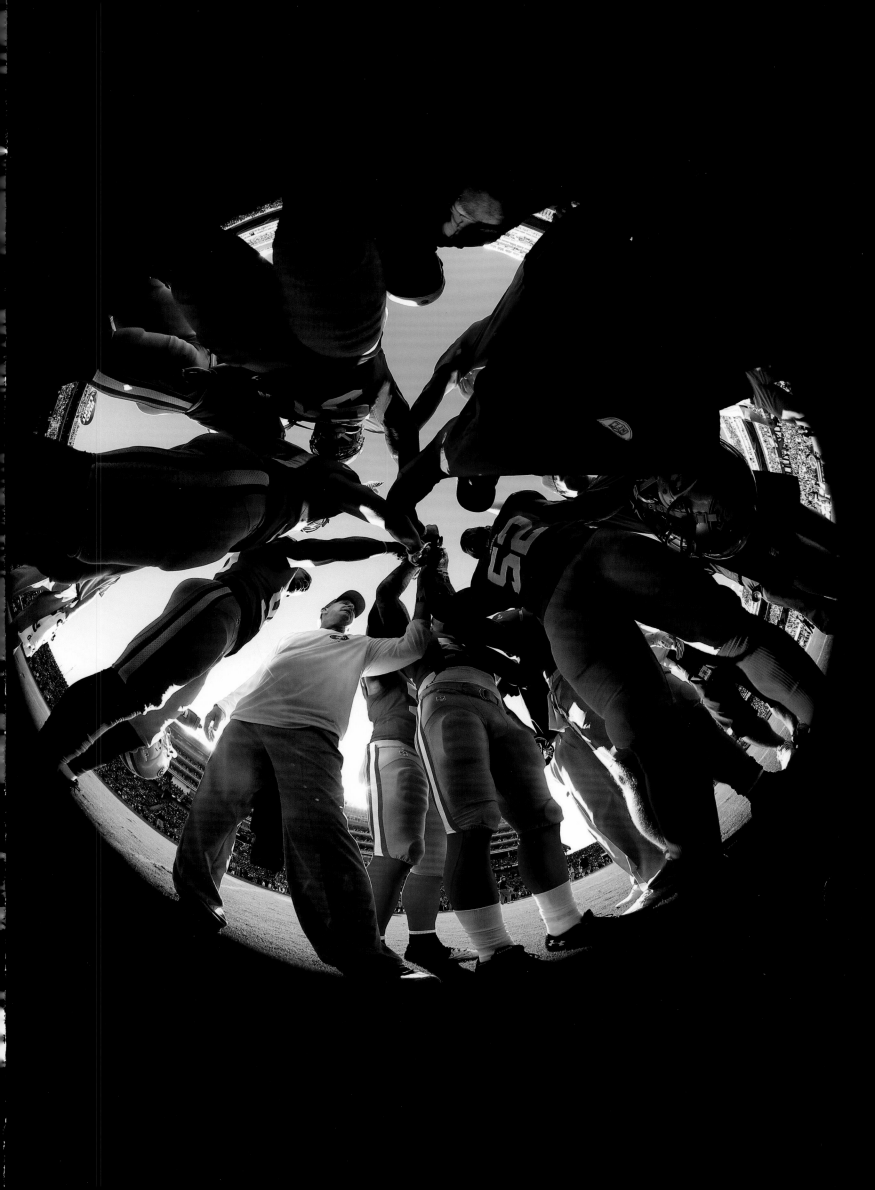

SAN FRANCISCO 49ERS

FROM KEZAR to LEVI'S STADIUM

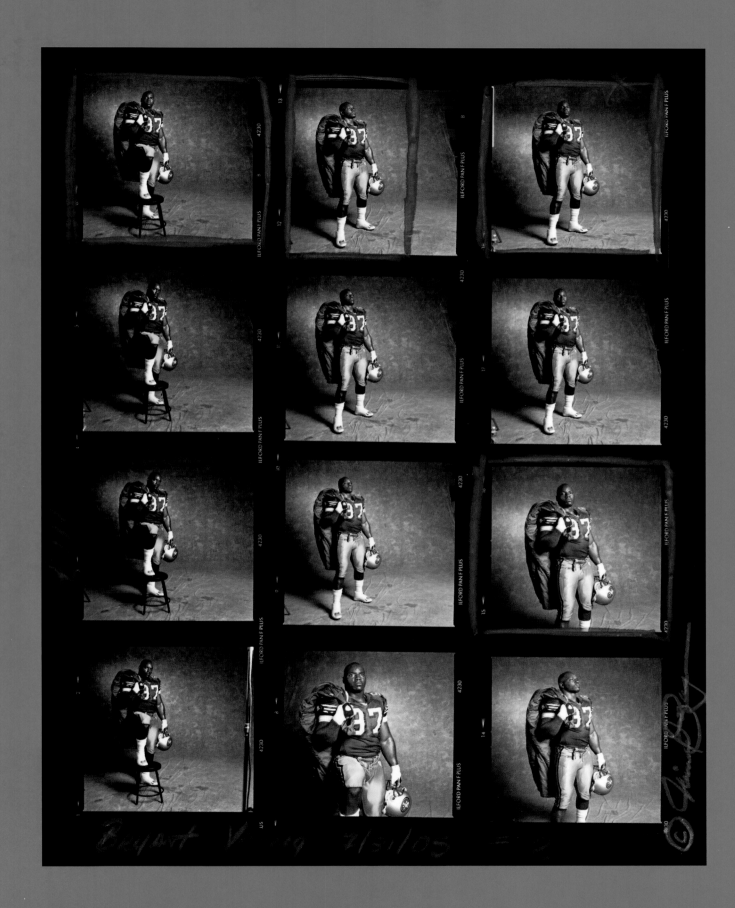

SAN FRANCISCO 49ERS

FROM KEZAR TO LEVI'S STADIUM

WRITTEN BY **BRIAN MURPHY**

FOREWORD BY **JERRY RICE**

INTRODUCTION BY **JED YORK**

INSIGHT EDITIONS

San Rafael, California

INSIGHT EDITIONS

PO Box 3088
San Rafael, CA 94912
www.insighteditions.com

 Find us on Facebook: www.facebook.com/InsightEditions

 Follow us on Twitter: @insighteditions

Library of Congress Cataloging-in-Publication Data available.

ISBN: 978-1-60887-436-1

PUBLISHER: Raoul Goff
CO-PUBLISHER: Michael Madden
ACQUISITIONS MANAGER: Steve Jones
EXECUTIVE EDITOR: Vanessa Lopez
PROJECT EDITOR: Dustin Jones
ART DIRECTOR: Chrissy Kwasnik
DESIGNER: Jon Glick
PRODUCTION EDITOR: Rachel Anderson
PRODUCTION MANAGER: Jane Chinn
PHOTO EDITOR: Michael Zagaris

ROOTS of PEACE   REPLANTED PAPER

Insight Editions, in association with Roots of Peace, will plant two trees
for each tree used in the manufacturing of this book. Roots of Peace is an
internationally renowned humanitarian organization dedicated to eradicating
land mines worldwide and converting war-torn lands into productive farms
and wildlife habitats. Roots of Peace will plant two million fruit and nut
trees in Afghanistan and provide farmers there with the skills and support
necessary for sustainable land use.

Manufactured in Hong Kong by Insight Editions

10 9 8 7 6 5 4 3 2 1

PAGES 1–2: Levi's Stadium on
opening day

PAGES 4–5: Joe Perry; Kezar Stadium,
September 17, 1950

PAGE 6: Ray Brown (left) and Steve
Wallace (right); NFC Playoff vs.
Green Bay Packers; January 4, 1997

PAGE 7: Bryan Young proof sheet,
July 31, 2005

PAGES 8–9: Defensive back Eric Wright
pregame in the Canton High School
locker room for the 1987 Hall of Fame
game vs. the Kansas City Chiefs

PAGE 10: Eric Wright exhausted and
dehydrated at halftime during a game
against the St. Louis Cardinals in 1983

PAGE 11: Ronnie Lott; American Bowl
Japan, August 7, 1989

PAGES 12–13: Bill Walsh and Joe
Montana; NFC Championship vs.
Chicago Bears, January 6, 1985.
Final score: Bears 0, 49ers 23

PAGE 14: Vernon Davis

PAGE 15: Colin Kaepernick celebrates his
touchdown scramble during Super Bowl
XLVII vs. Baltimore Ravens

PAGES 16–17: Levi's Stadium;
preseason game vs. Denver Broncos,
August 17, 2014

PAGES 20–21: Kendall Hunter leaps for a
touchdown vs. Tampa Bay Buccaneers,
December 15, 2013

PAGES 24–25: Justin Smith (left) and
Patrick Willis (right)

CONTENTS

FOREWORD BY
JERRY RICE

I HAD A CHANCE to tour Levi's Stadium with Steve Young before it opened—it was unbelievable—and we both talked about the idea of playing football there, about how playing on that field would feel like we had died and gone to heaven. It's so beautiful and perfect. It's the sort of stadium I dreamed about when I was a player.

Now, I'm not saying I didn't enjoy Candlestick Park! But to be able to perform in a high-profile stadium like Levi's Stadium would be a dream come true. The new guys on the 49ers will be able to make their mark there, start their dynasty.

I like everything about the stadium: the suites in the SAP Tower, the food—with everything from franks and pizza to curry and vegetarian dishes. Man, when I see options like that even I have some fun. I give myself a day to come to the stadium, eat whatever I want, drink a beer, but then the next day, you know I have to get right back into my routine! And that locker room. You could play a football game in that locker room!

The idea of building a new stadium was something we talked about for years, back when I was playing. Eddie DeBartolo fought hard for it back in the 1990s, and the team finally got it done with Santa Clara.

It's interesting to think of how different Candlestick Park was from the new home of the 49ers. The locker rooms at the 'Stick were small. The field was wet. You had to deal with the wind. But to be honest, I think that gave us a little edge. We knew our footing, we knew the ball would blow a certain way in certain wind conditions. At Levi's Stadium, the field won't be wet and slippery, that's for sure. The pristine conditions will get the 49ers hyped to put on good performances and set the stage for some historic games.

That's one of the most exciting things about Levi's Stadium—looking at this immaculate football temple and imagining the historic performances that are destined to unfold here. But it's also great to see the way the 49ers are celebrating their history, even while looking forward. I'm very excited about the museum and Hall of Fame at Levi's Stadium. To have all the memorabilia from different players and to be reminded of the great tradition of the San Francisco 49ers and all that we've accomplished is awesome.

They've even made statues out of some of us 49ers Hall of Fame players. Wow. It's a little eerie to see a statue of yourself, but it's such an honor, such a huge compliment. I really enjoyed playing the game, loved the game, loved entertaining the fans and working with my teammates to break so many records. My plan before the stadium opened was to take a picture of my statue and me first thing and then put it on social media!

The big thing, though, is that the 49ers new legacy is going to be here, at Levi's Stadium. The 49ers understand everything we accomplished at Candlestick, but this is their new home. If anything, it will make them hungrier to get it done, to create their own legacy.

And don't forget, Super Bowl 50 is coming in 2016. Imagine what that could be like: the San Francisco 49ers taking the field at Levi's Stadium for Super Bowl 50. Talk about a dream come true.

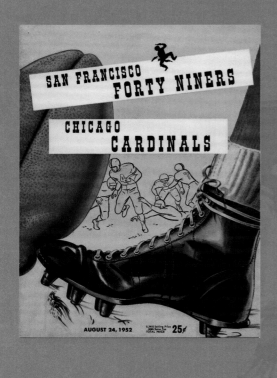

SAN FRANCISCO **FORTY NINERS**

CHICAGO **CARDINALS**

AUGUST 24, 1952   25¢

May 2, 1925: Kezar Stadium opened.

1940: First-ever major college football double-header is played at Kezar, which features the Stanford Indians vs. the San Francisco Dons and the Santa Clara Broncos vs. the Utah State Aggies.

1954: The San Francisco 49ers establish the "Million Dollar Backfield," composed of quarterback Y. A. Tittle and running backs Joe Perry, Hugh McElhenny, and John Henry Johnson.

October 27, 1957: Owner Tony Morabito suddenly dies of a heart attack during a 49ers-Bears game. Down 17-7 at that point, the team rallies to win the game 21-17.

1925 1930 1935 1940 1945 1950 1955 1960 1965

1928: Kezar hosts city high school championship football game between San Francisco Polytechnic and Lowell. More than 50,000 attended.

September 8, 1946: The San Francisco 49ers lose to the New York Yankees in the first-ever regular-season pro football game at Kezar.

December 22, 1957: The San Francisco 49ers play their first NFL playoff game at Kezar Stadium against the Detroit Lions, blowing a 24-7 lead to lose 27-24.

January 20, 1985: The 49ers take their second Super Bowl win against the Miami Dolphins in Super Bowl XIX.

April 19, 2012: Groundbreaking ceremony at Levi's Stadium, commencing a heroic construction effort.

January 22, 1989: The 49ers take their third Super Bowl win against the Cincinnati Bengals in Super Bowl XXIII.

January 3, 1971: The 49ers face off against the Dallas Cowboys at Kezar for the NFC Championship. The Cowboys outlast the 49ers, winning 17-10.

December 23, 2013: The 49ers last game at Candlestick Park, where they take a 34-24 win over the Atlanta Falcons, punctuated by NaVorro Bowman's "Pick at the 'Stick."

January 28, 1990: The 49ers take their fourth Super Bowl win against the Denver Broncos in Super Bowl XXIV.

October 10, 1971: The San Francisco 49ers play their first game at Candlestick Park.

January 29, 1995: The 49ers take their fifth Super Bowl win against the San Diego Chargers in Super Bowl XXIX.

1975   1980   1985   1990   1995   2000   2005   2010   2015

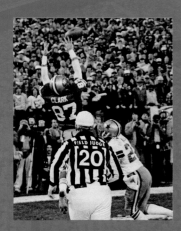

January 10, 1982: The 49ers face the Dallas Cowboys in the NFC Championship at Candlestick. Joe Montana connects with Dwight Clark for "The Catch."

July 17, 2014: Eight hundred and nineteen days after the 49ers and the Santa Clara Stadium Authority celebrated the groundbreaking, Levi's Stadium is officially opened.

January 24, 1982: The 49ers take their first Super Bowl win against the Cincinnati Bengals in Super Bowl XVI.

August 2, 2014: San Jose Earthquakes play Seattle Sounders in the first sporting event at Levi's Stadium.

August 17, 2014: The 49ers host the Denver Broncos in the first NFL preseason game ever at Levi's Stadium.

August 24, 2014: Backup quarterback Blaine Gabbert links up with tight end Vance McDonald for the first 49ers touchdown at Levi's Stadium during the preseason game against the San Diego Chargers.

September 14, 2014: 49ers vs. Chicago Bears in the first-ever regular season NFL game at Levi's Stadium.

INTRODUCTION BY
JED YORK

I DON'T REMEMBER EVER NOT BEING INVOLVED WITH THE 49ERS. My family bought the team before I was born. And I was born in 1981, the season of the 49ers first Super Bowl. I guess I was good luck. I remember going to my first game in 1984 in Cleveland and sitting on Jennifer Montana's lap. And there's a picture of my uncle, Eddie DeBartolo Jr.; Bill Walsh; and me hanging in the lobby of our team headquarters that was taken in Pittsburgh in 1987.

The 49ers were a constant. It was always Summerall and Madden on TV every Sunday at 4 o'clock, and I remember watching those games from my boyhood home in Youngstown, Ohio. We had a pretty big side yard, so we'd watch football, and at halftime my little brother and I would go out there and reenact the game.

I remember my grandfather would come to our house for dinner, and my mom would cook spaghetti and meatballs, and the TV would show a segment on the 49ers. So you'd have my family members around the table, and my uncle would be on TV talking about trying to win a Super Bowl, and it was just normal. I think that's why the stage never felt too big for me. The stage had always been there since I was a kid. And I watched how my grandfather handled things. He was very cool, calm, and collected, but always very passionate.

Early on, I got a sense of how important it was to win and how important it was to be a good part of the community. Even though I never saw that in San Francisco until my teens, the connection was there, and I realized how significant it was to have a team that represented the community that celebrated them. My family knows this is a great asset, and I thought I could continue the legacy and tradition my grandfather, uncle, and mother started and help take that legacy to a future we'd all been dreaming of for a long time.

As far back as the '80s and '90s, my uncle had been pushing for a new stadium, well before he won a ballot measure in 1997. Candlestick wasn't really built for football, originally, and the additions required to make it football-ready didn't really provide the best fan experience. Candlestick provided a lot of great memories, a lot of moments people will never forget and wouldn't change for the world, but it never provided a great fan experience. Getting food, going to the restroom, getting in and out of Candlestick—that was never really a first-class experience. We have a first-class football team and have long wanted a stadium that mirrors that.

From the start, The Santa Clara Stadium Authority (SCSA) and the 49ers wanted the new stadium to represent the Bay Area. When you look at a lot of new buildings, they're bigger, flashier, more expensive. What we wanted Levi's Stadium to be was smarter—whether that means building technology-forward or making sure that we were functionally green. That's what the Bay Area has always represented. With that in mind, Levi's Stadium is the first net neutral stadium in North or South America, and 100 percent of our energy comes from the sun—that's just smart, plain and simple.

It's easy to put solar panels up. But SCSA and the 49ers wanted to be functionally green, to make the green roof (known as the NRG Solar Terrace) multipurpose rather than just a place to put the solar panels and provide one of the most unique views in all of sports. Thought went into

OPPOSITE: Jed York at Levi's Stadium groundbreaking ceremony

every aspect of the building, and this unique space signifies that. Not only does it capture the sun's power and put it back into the building, but it's a place where you can enjoy the game, have a beer, have a party during non-NFL events. It's one of the signature areas of Levi's Stadium.

In reimagining what stadium gastronomy could look like, we took inspiration from the great food and wine culture the Bay Area has to offer. We realized we didn't want to ship in frozen hot dogs when we could source local, organic beef to make fresh franks. Similarly, we took advantage of the great wines of Napa and Sonoma—some of the best wine in the world is produced right in our backyards—and put a lot of effort and emphasis into building that into the stadium experience.

The 49ers and SCSA wanted to create a unique, interactive stadium experience. In doing so we again chose IQ over flashiness. We didn't want to integrate technology for technology's sake, but we did want to make sure that if you have a smartphone, it can act as your all-access pass to a game. From your phone, you can upload your parking. You can upload your tickets. And if you want to transfer your tickets to somebody, it's a quick, easy transfer. We realized we had the opportunity to be a ticketless, cashless building where you could park, enter the stadium, and order franks, fries, and sodas to your seat with nothing in your pocket but your smartphone. We know this will be an ever-evolving stadium—again like the innovative culture that defines the Bay Area. Our modern mobile devices can be used in a coffee shop to shoot out an e-mail or a tweet, and we realized we'd be behind the curve if we didn't introduce that into Levi's Stadium. That drove our vision of in-stadium Wi-Fi.

We know there are sixteen different cameras shooting a game. We should be able to give fans the opportunity to see a few of those different camera angles, so they can check out the replay they want—and that drove our vision for including instant replay in the Stadium App; that, and the tireless pursuit of creating the most immersive, innovative, and exciting in-stadium experience possible.

Equally important as giving our fans the best experience possible is giving our team a home it can thrive in. For as long as I can remember, the 49ers essentially had sixteen road games a year. Playing at Candlestick, they had to transfer everything from their practice facility to the stadium, and it wasn't an easy logistical experience for our guys. Here at Levi's Stadium, the athletes will be in their locker room all year—no transferring gear back and forth. And the training facility is literally fifteen feet away from the stadium. It makes it a lot simpler for our guys—they know their environment and know where they're going to work every day, whether it be game day or practice.

Where these two things dovetail—fan experience and player experience—is in the configuration of the stadium. We wanted the fans lower and closer to the field than they were at Candlestick. Building the suites on one side of the stadium allowed us to bring the upper deck down significantly, ensuring there wouldn't be a "nosebleed" seat in the house. We also created an immense lower bowl so we could put as many fans as possible as close to the action as possible. This gets fans involved in the action, and involved fans make for pumped-up athletes. Two-thirds of our fans will be in the lower bowl, for a much louder stadium and significantly more intimate experience.

As for the name, obviously it's going to be an iconic building in Northern California. It was bound to host Super Bowls and other major events. But we wanted to make sure we worked with a brand that fit our vision. When you talk about the original miner 49ers, Levi's was their original partner. I don't think you can have a better fit for a naming rights partner.

But all the finer points aside, Levi's Stadium is a blank canvas. It's up to this team and the 68,500 fans that come to the games on Sundays to really make this place a historic milestone in football.

Jed York with younger brother Tony in their 49ers gear

The building's statement is clean and innovative. It's open, airy. We're talking about Northern California, where you can be outside much of the year, and we want to take advantage of that. On a clear day, you can see downtown San Francisco from the green roof, and it's easy to see downtown San Jose. And when you look at the stadium, it looks like it fits. It blends into the surroundings, but you also know that it's different, something special.

But of all the unique features of Levi's Stadium, I think my favorite part of it is the museum. It's innovative and interactive—a trademark of the stadium as a whole—but also a profound celebration of the history and legacy of the 49ers. All of our 49ers Hall-of-Famers have their own lifelike, life-size statue in an iconic pose. Gordy Soltau is kicking, Jerry Rice is scoring a touchdown, Bill Walsh is in his typical Walsh pose, and my uncle and grandfather are both holding the Lombardi Trophy in the pose they assumed after the 1984 Super Bowl.

We also worked with Bill Walsh's son, Craig, to get his memorabilia together and re-create his office. We have his coaching tapes, and we do cutups of Bill teaching the plays and showing how they worked in games. We wanted to give people the opportunity to not just read a plaque, but really have an immersive experience.

I never got to see the Million Dollar Backfield. But here in the 49ers Museum presented by Sony, you're able to go see those guys in action—not just read about them—watch them in short films and really experience what they brought to the game. I was fortunate to grow up in the 1980s and be a part of all those Super Bowl championships, but think about my son. He'll never watch Joe or Jerry or Ronnie play. But he'll be able to see it and feel it and experience it in the museum. I can't think of anything better than that. And we celebrate guys like Hall of Fame defensive back Jimmy Johnson. From a historical standpoint, he should be on a pedestal. Those guys, who didn't have the championships, who played at a high level of football, those were amazing teams, and it's important to see that, experience it, celebrate it, and to know there is more to the 49ers than the dynasty that unfolded in the 1980s.

We want to take advantage of the great history of the 49ers, but we want the museum to be more than that. We want it to be a real learning center for the youth in the Bay Area. To use something that's fun, like football, to teach science, technology, engineering, math. To be able to show kids: This is how you create a green building. This is how Joe Montana was able to throw a pass and Jerry Rice was able to catch it. Here, we're able to get kids excited about sports and in turn get them excited about learning.

My mom has always been focused on giving kids an opportunity to enhance their lives through education. This is a place where we will be able to inspire kids. I think sports, and our players, definitely do a great job of inspiring. But taking the next step is important. You might not be the next Frank Gore or Colin Kaepernick, but we want to translate the excitement and enthusiasm our team inspires into a greater drive to excel—not only in sports but in everything. That's what the museum educational facility is all about: showing kids that a career path in science, technology, engineering, and math can really be their ticket to a great life and an inspired future.

But all the finer points aside, Levi's Stadium is a blank canvas. It's up to this team and the 68,500 fans that come to the games on Sundays to really make this place a historic milestone in football. We've been given the opportunity to start something new, a new chapter in the already legendary story of the 49ers. I'm looking forward to seeing the traditions that emerge and develop here, what our fans push for and celebrate. I'm excited to see that start from the ground level and really build on the great legacy of the San Francisco 49ers. And I'm excited to think about a future filled with great football from our boys in the red and gold.

CHAPTER ONE

BREAKING GROUND

-50 | 40- | 30- | 20- | 10-

What you see now when the 49ers take to their home field at Levi's Stadium—an open-air, exposed-beam stadium with a field of lush natural grass surrounded by luxuriously wide concourses and served by cutting-edge technology in a progressive, environmentally friendly atmosphere—was not always that way.

The very spot where Levi's Stadium stands was once a weedy, cracked, cragged, and empty patch of concrete where the Santa Clara Police Department would conduct vehicular training for its officers.

Talk about having a vision.

This vision transformed what was once an obscure corner of a parking lot behind Great America amusement park—a place most Santa Clara residents probably never knew existed, much less 49ers fans across Northern California—into the scintillating new home of one of the NFL's most glamorous franchises.

Niners fans were accustomed to watching their team play home games at crowded, damp, and outdated Candlestick Park, the oldest nonrenovated stadium in the league. Upon entering Levi's Stadium in 2014, their expectations weren't just exceeded, their minds were blown, largely because of the central goal pithily proclaimed by team owner Dr. John York to his crew of architects and engineers at the outset of planning in 2006. "I want this stadium to be the first of the next generation," York challenged his audience. "Not the last stadium of the previous generation." This aim to create a next-generation stadium required more than just boardroom spitballing. It required bold action and adventurous execution.

PAGES 38–39: Levi's Stadium groundbreaking ceremony

THESE PAGES: Architecture firm HNTB's detailed, full-color renderings reveal the ambitious vision for Levi's Stadium.

Levi's Stadium, futuristic and accessible all at once, exists because many arrows pointed the Bay Area's oldest homegrown professional sports franchise here—the first was the expiration date on Candlestick Park. While the old concrete bowl just off Highway 101 at the southeastern tip of San Francisco had been home to many of the NFL's greatest players, games, and memories of the past thirty-plus years, the proliferation of twenty-first-century comforts and experience-enhancing features in professional sports arenas made Candlestick look tired and ancient.

Put it this way: Not every NFL team had to deal with cramped locker rooms, broken elevators, the odd power outage, and if rains came, floating porta-potties in its parking lot. All these problems gnawed at 49ers chief executive officer Jed York. York had grown up in the family business knowing Candlestick Park held plenty of memories, but he also knew it didn't hold the key to a successful future for the 49ers.

In the salary-cap NFL, revenue for signing bonuses is king. The 49ers gazed enviously at new stadiums with state-of-the-art club areas and suites that enabled teams to rake in dollars that could go toward roster enhancement. The way the 49ers saw it, they were handicapped at Candlestick. Stadiums were the "key differential," in the words of team president Paraag Marathe, between high-revenue and low-revenue teams.

> What was once an obscure corner of a parking lot behind Great America amusement park— a place most Santa Clara residents probably never knew existed, much less 49ers fans across Northern California— [became the] home of one of the NFL's most glamorous franchises.

The 49ers had been seeking to replace Candlestick Park since the 1990s. In 1997, then-owner Eddie DeBartolo Jr. put a ballot measure to the voters of San Francisco to build a new stadium/mall project on Hunters Point, near the site of the 'Stick. The measure passed, but many hurdles tripped up the project, including the transfer of ownership from DeBartolo Jr. to his sister and her husband, Denise DeBartolo York and Dr. John York.

The Yorks took over, still intent on replacing Candlestick. They restarted talks with San Francisco about a project on Hunters Point, but negotiations stalled. Then, in the fall of 2006, convinced that the difficulty of building in California's intricate marketplace demanded the most reasonable solution, and after exploring more than eighty different potential sites, the Yorks made the big move: The 49ers announced their intention to seek a partnership with Santa Clara to build a stadium, 40 miles south of San Francisco and adjacent to the SAP Performance Facility, where the team had practiced since 1988.

The reasons were clear. Santa Clara was a more willing partner than the city and county of San Francisco. The land was easier to build on. And access and transportation to the stadium would be dramatically improved. The new stadium would be surrounded by the heavy-rail Capitol Corridor Amtrak train, by light rail from along the Peninsula, and by Highways 101, 237, and 880, with thirteen interchanges between them. Even the thoroughfares surrounding the park, like Great America Parkway, were four-to-eight lanes, making them wider and more accommodating than the streets, like Jamestown Avenue, used to access Candlestick Park.

Dr. John York, the 49ers co-chairman, said the variables added up to a lightning-bolt moment. "The interstates . . . the interchanges . . . the wide roads . . . all of a sudden you envision a stadium that has light rail 50 feet from the entrance, and heavy rail within a five-minute walk," Dr. York said. "And you hit yourself in the forehead and say: Why didn't I listen to the Santa Clara city planners all along? They built the idea for this thirty years ago."

View of Levi's Stadium from
Great America amusement park

Moreover, the 49ers felt a connection to the area. Team headquarters had been located in Santa Clara for a quarter century. As Levi's Stadium was built, workers measured the nearest distance from the stadium to the practice facility. It was 13½ feet. "It just made too much sense," said Marathe. Though at first building in Santa Clara seemed unlikely, it became highly logical.

NFL commissioner Roger Goodell was one of the site's earliest proponents. In order to convince the league's Park Avenue headquarters that this was a viable solution for the team, the 49ers and then Santa Clara mayor Patricia Mahan gave Goodell a tour. Saving the best for last, they took him on the 200-foot-high "Sky Tower" ride at adjacent Great America amusement park. Mahan had the ride operator move the 360-degree ride at a slower speed, so she could point out all the positives of the infrastructure below. There, 200 feet above the ground, Goodell turned to Mahan as they circled and said: "This is a no-brainer."

"Plus," Mahan said with a laugh, "we gave him a 'Santa Clara' sweatshirt." Nothing like a piece of cozy regional merchandise to help seal the deal.

But saying you want to build a stadium in Santa Clara is one thing. Convincing the voters to approve the project is another. In California's budget-strained cities, leverage is on the side of the voter. Prominent watchdog groups have made land giveaways and sweetheart deals relics from another era. The 49ers were entering into a den of skepticism where they had to prove themselves and their intentions to the city of Santa Clara.

Two years of negotiations with the Santa Clara City Council and with Mayor Mahan finally resulted in a ballot measure in the spring of 2010. Voters were asked the following question: "Shall the City of Santa Clara adopt Ordinance 17.20 leasing City property for a professional football stadium and other events; no use of City General or Enterprise funds for construction; no new taxes for residents for stadium; Redevelopment Agency funds capped for construction; private party pays all construction cost overruns; no City/Agency obligation for stadium operating/maintenance; private party payment of projected fair market rent; and additional funds for senior/youth/library/recreation to City's General Fund?"

Jed York hoped to convince voters to answer that question in the affirmative. Thus began "Jed's Great Adventure," in which a young man in his late twenties, the grandson of family scion Ed DeBartolo Sr., carrying on his family's four-decade legacy, did something decidedly unromantic and old-school.

Jed knocked on doors. He sat in living rooms. He listened to doubters. He encouraged supporters. He knocked on more doors. He sat in more living rooms. He sold his idea, over and over, one person at a time. He joked to skeptics: "If you don't think I'm serious about this, ask yourself why I, a twenty-nine-year-old bachelor, am spending Friday night, not out in San Francisco with friends and family, but in your living room stating our case?"

Finally, election night came. Much like his uncle in San Francisco in 1997, Jed won the vote. A total of 14,782 Santa Clara residents voted "yes," while a total of 10,505 voted "no." With 58.2 percent of Santa Clarans approving the stadium, the 49ers had the green light to build. Unlike the 1997 plan in San Francisco, however, this one would reach fruition. Team history was changing, right before the Bay Area's eyes.

Current Santa Clara Mayor Jamie Matthews

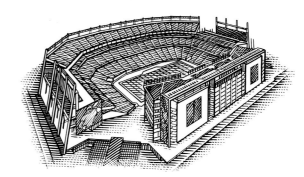

The 49ers and the Santa Clara Stadium Authority set about hiring San Francisco–based HNTB as architects, and they hired Turner/Devcon—a joint construction firm formed by New York–based Turner and Milpitas-based Devcon—as the contractors. Devcon had a rich history with the 49ers. Its owner, Gary Filizetti, was close to Eddie DeBartolo Jr. and had the contract to build on Hunters Point after the 1997 election. Devcon built the Santa Clara practice facility in 1987, and Filizetti was an old football player from— where else?—Santa Clara University. They call that "foreshadowing" in the literary world.

All that was well and good, but in a capitalist economy, money is what turns plans into reality. The stadium would cost just shy of $1 billion, and needed bank loans. This would require a game plan, an airtight argument to New York banks that $850 million was worth loaning to a team named the *San Francisco* 49ers that wanted to build its stadium 40.1 miles south of Candlestick Park.

Jed York again saddled up, this time with his colleague Gideon Yu, a former high-ranking executive with Facebook, YouTube, and Yahoo. Yu had agreed to fly to New York to help pitch the new stadium.

In December 2011, the SCSA and the 49ers succeeded, securing a loan of $850 million, the largest ever in professional sports. The NFL, remembering Goodell's Great America ride, would add a $200 million loan of their own.

Exuberant, York and Yu flew back to the Bay Area, fully intent on helping Santa Clara build not just a new place to play, but an innovative, interactive, green, and aesthetically attractive stadium. SCSA and the 49ers had the land. They had the builders. And they had the money. They had all they needed to put their vision into action. All that was missing was a name.

In today's sports world, revenue from naming rights can be a huge boon. And for companies looking to expand their brand, the boon can be mutual. Of course, the 49ers had experienced the downside of naming rights: as the

TOP: Levi's Stadium groundbreaking ceremony

ABOVE: Levi's president & CEO Chip Bergh

OPPOSITE: From left to right: Dr. John York, Jed York, 49ers executive VP Patty Inglis, and Denise DeBartolo York

team switched their stadium's name from Candlestick Park to 3Com Park to Monster Park and back to Candlestick Park in the span of just fifteen years, they learned that temporary flings with companies can frustrate fans. The team hoped the SCSA could find a clean connection with a brand that was both culturally and symbolically relevant.

In their San Francisco offices, Levi's president and CEO Chip Bergh and Levi's Brand president James Curleigh had an idea: What if San Francisco's 150-year-old blue jeans brand, worn by the original, "real" 49ers, the gold-rush Californians, connected itself to the future of the NFL's 49ers?

Put simply, Levi's pitched to the SCSA that the 49ers mascot, Sourdough Sam, is the kind of guy who should be wearing Levi's.

The SCSA and the 49ers agreed. In May 2013, Levi's and the SCSA signed a twenty-year, $220-million deal and put a clean red Levi's "batwing" logo on the suite tower, announcing that this was now Levi's Stadium and putting their new home's name on the tips of 49ers fans' tongues before it even opened.

Exuberant, York and Yu flew back to the Bay Area, fully intent on helping Santa Clara build not just a new stadium, but an innovative, green, attractive stadium. SCSA and the 49ers had the land. They had the builders. And they had the money. Now, all they needed to do was put their vision into action.

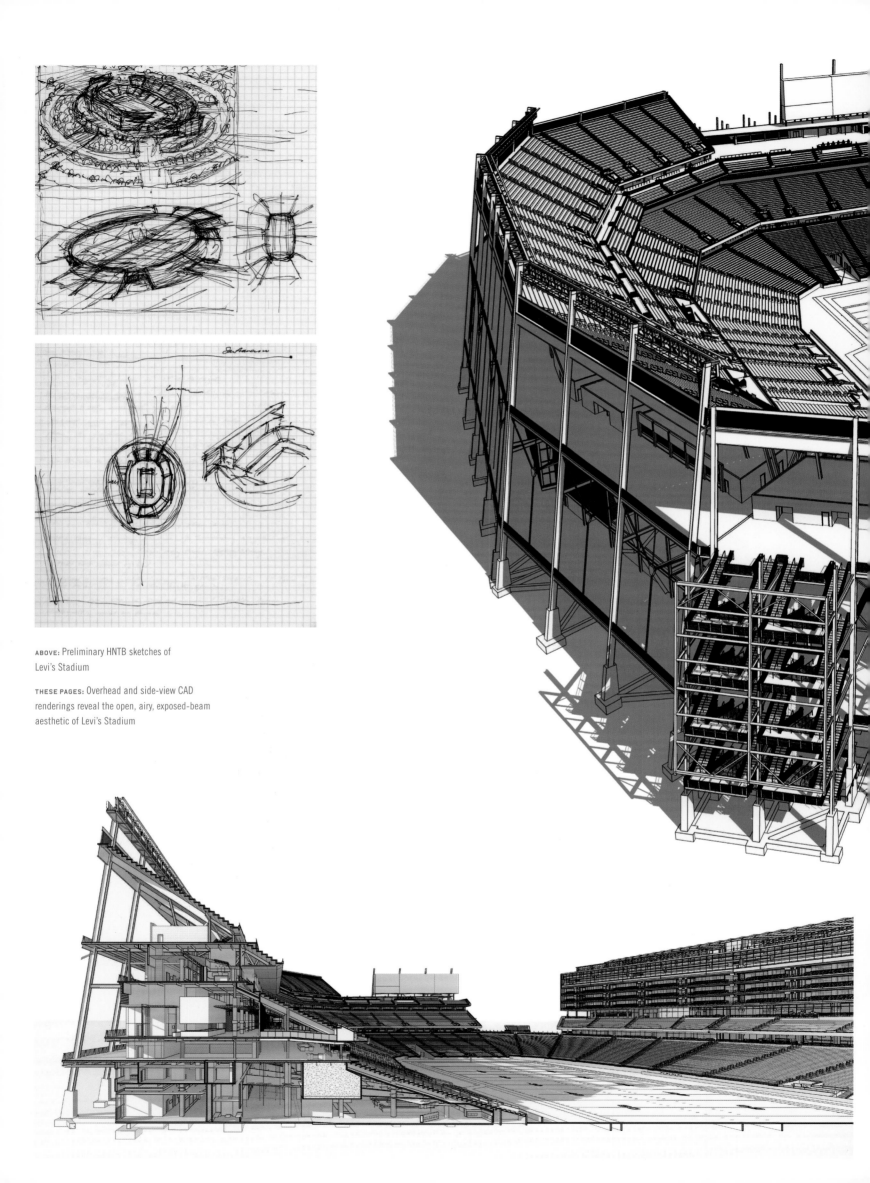

ABOVE: Preliminary HNTB sketches of
Levi's Stadium

THESE PAGES: Overhead and side-view CAD
renderings reveal the open, airy, exposed-beam
aesthetic of Levi's Stadium

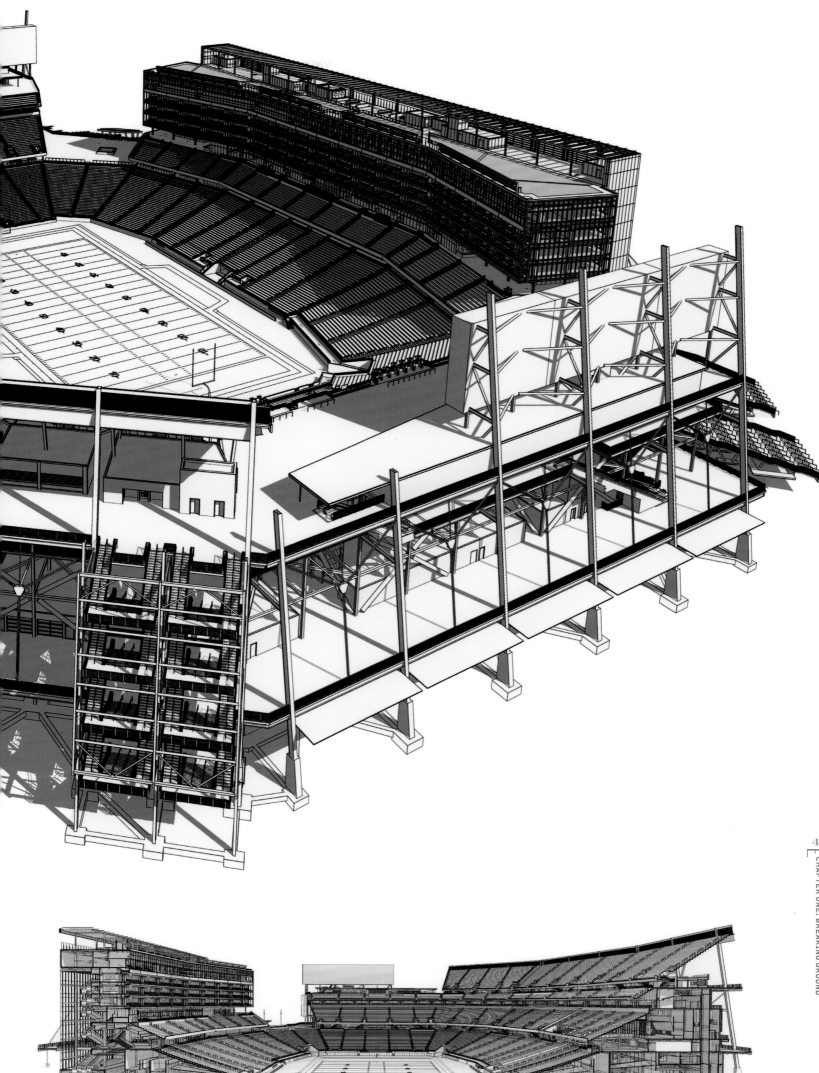

On April 19, 2012, the SCSA broke ground, with its board members and Denise DeBartolo York, Dr. John York, Jed York, and his siblings Tony, Mara, and Jenna York, and 49ers coach Jim Harbaugh all posing for pictures, holding shovels and wearing hard hats. Harbaugh, never short on hyperbole, declared, "I see a team building with a shovel in one hand and a sword in the other."

Jed York wasn't quite as dramatic. He made a joke about increasing the number of women's restrooms at Levi's Stadium, drawing a cheer, and kept it simple. "I want this to be a showcase of technology that enhances the game experience," he said. "And I want it to be something unique to Northern California."

On April 23, 2012, the SCSA turned the project over to Turner/Devcon, and the massive building project began. The project employed 900 workers daily, with sometimes up to 1,200 workers on site. It used 22,000 tons of structural steel in the main structure. Working twenty-four hours a day to get the foundation in, crews installed 30 miles of deep electrical conduit and plumbing pipe. Nearly 90,000 cubic yards of concrete were poured. And to Jed's earlier point, they built 1,135 "water closets," as vice president of Devcon Construction, Jonathan Harvey, said with a laugh—250 more than at Candlestick Park.

As the engineers, architects, and contractors studied the site, bordered by Tasman Drive to the north, the Silicon Valley Power station to the south, the 49ers SAP Performance Facility and Santa Clara Youth Soccer Park to the east, and San Tomas Aquino Creek to the west, they noticed the site was a tight, small footprint, clearly defining their workspace.

Drier soil conditions were easier to work with in Santa Clara than at Hunters Point. Foundation piles didn't need to go nearly as deep in Santa

Clara. Think of it as the difference between hammering a stake in dry, hard dirt versus hammering a stake in mud. The area's infrastructure, with public transportation, freeways, and approximately thirty thousand parking spots within walking distance, surpassed Candlestick Park, which featured eighteen thousand parking spaces and no light or heavy-rail connections. All told, the contractors and architects said, it was a "very inviting location," according to Harvey.

With the stage set, development moved even faster than imagined. The plan initially was to open for the 2015 season. But everyone thought, *What are we waiting for?* Team executive vice president Larry MacNeil called the Turner/Devcon crew in the fall of 2011 and said, "Let's open in 2014. You up for this?"

Harvey, who'd been involved in the 49ers original Hunters Point project in 1997, laughed and said: "I've been involved in this project for fifteen years, and now you're going to make me go fast?"

THESE PAGES: The construction effort in building Levi's Stadium was nothing short of heroic. The crews of up to 1,200 a day employed 22,000 tons of structural steel, installed 30 miles of electrical conduit and plumbing pipe, and poured nearly 90,000 cubic yards of concrete.

PAGES 50–51: Levi's Stadium as it came together from a vacant parking lot to one of the Bay Area's most iconic buildings

Every roll of the dice worked for the 49ers and the SCSA. They set a twenty-six-month construction schedule, starting in April 2012, and nailed it.

OPPOSITE: Topping out SAP Tower; the last two beams were painted in 49ers gold.

ABOVE (TOP ROW): Solar panels and the NRG Solar Terrace were a key component to Levi's Stadium earning a LEED gold certification. (MIDDLE ROW): Installation of the commemorative bricks that line the Levi's Stadium plaza and display the Faithful's contribution toward the building of the stadium (BOTTOM ROW): Field goal installation

This is where all the positives of building in Santa Clara seemed to work exponentially. As project executive Jack Hill noted, the site had great weather, great partnership from the Santa Clara Stadium Authority, proximity to materials, and perhaps most importantly, could draw from the Bay Area's skilled and deep labor pool. The SCSA and the 49ers knew that many of the big Silicon Valley tech firms were planning major construction projects in the next few years, and those projects would dip into the same labor market they were counting on. The time to build was now, and the way to build was quickly.

Still, moving up the completion date by a year meant they had to "phase" its permitting from Santa Clara. In other words, they would start building some of the stadium before all the drawings were done, creating a bit of overlap between design and construction, but every roll of the dice worked for the 49ers and the SCSA. They set a twenty-six-month construction schedule, starting in April 2012, and nailed it.

"We said: Let's see if we can't embark on this," explained Hill. "We took some risks, but everything fell on our side. It was a combination of skill and luck."

Jonathan Harvey, from Devcon, concurred. "You have a very sophisticated construction market," he said. "You have the cream of the crop when it comes to design and build. You have creative engineers and consultants that come with the package. You have a motivated and productive workforce." All that talent set to work on completing the vision, starting with the SAP Tower.

TOP: SAP Tower during seat installation

OPPOSITE: The NRG Solar Terrace (top) sits atop the SAP Tower and its luxury suites (bottom).

When in medical school in Chicago, Dr. John York used to take walks around the Windy City and marvel at its architecture. He studied it, gazing for hours. "I've always had," he said, "a big interest in spaces." This passion for buildings would be the seedling for Dr. York's primary vision at Levi's Stadium.

Today, the red seats and stark white exterior make for a color scheme that dominates Levi's Stadium. It lets opponents know they are in hostile territory—49ers territory. But the defining architectural masterstroke of Levi's Stadium is Dr. York's brainchild, the suite tower (now SAP Tower).

When the stadium was being designed, Dr. York counted only a few features as essential, and having the largest lower bowl possible was one of them. He noticed that in other new stadiums, with expanding suites in mezzanine levels, lower bowls were shrinking, and upper decks, which placed fans far from the action, were expanding. He did not want that to happen at Levi's Stadium. Building a suite tower was key to that idea. By stacking seven levels of suites, clubs, and a press box on the west side of the structure, they were able to maximize the number of seats close to the field and get more fans fully engaged with the action. This design eliminated an upper deck on the west side and created more seats in the lower bowl. While some suites sit on the east side of the stadium, 103 of the 170 suites are in the suite tower. Thus, they essentially removed the mezzanine "suite layer" that can make fans in the upper deck feel like they're miles away from the field.

In essence, three sides of the stadium are pure seating for a pure football experience. As per Dr. York's original vision, they wanted a "collegiate feel," said Lanson Nichols, vice president of the architectural firm HNTB, "and the largest lower bowl possible."

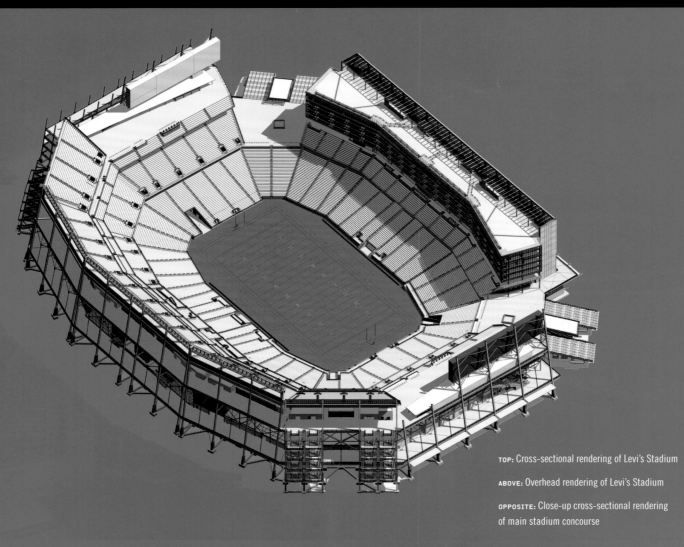

TOP: Cross-sectional rendering of Levi's Stadium

ABOVE: Overhead rendering of Levi's Stadium

OPPOSITE: Close-up cross-sectional rendering of main stadium concourse

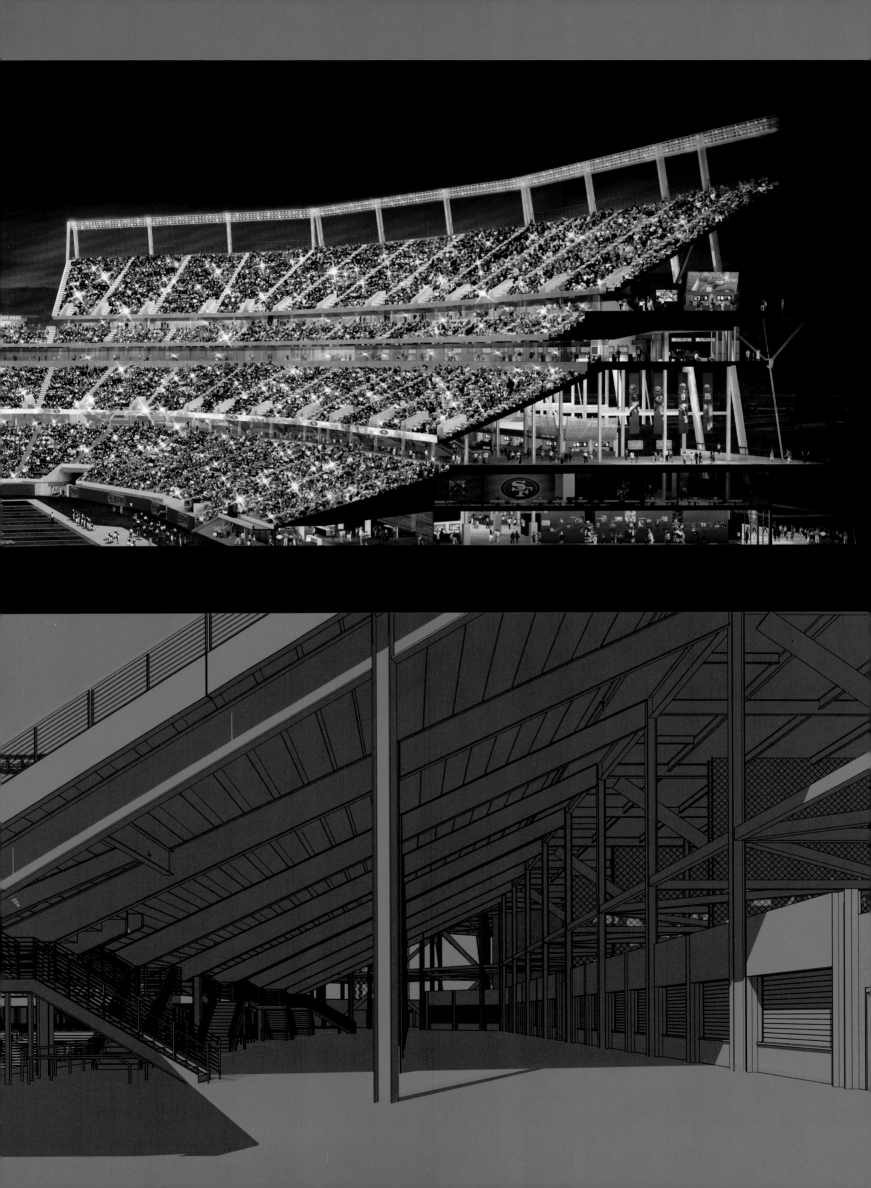

As they built the suite tower, the construction and design team could see the trademark aspect of Levi's Stadium begin to form, even before a game was played. This would be an intimate environment, they noted. And the suite tower, they believed, would be something that future stadiums would copy, standing the test of time.

SAP Tower also enabled the 49ers and SCSA to place all suites between the goal lines, making them easier to sell. No more need to try and sell end-zone suites with less-desirable views. Placing all the suites together also concentrated manpower, a huge step toward conserving energy and resources for the green-conscious stadium. SAP Tower's unique design opened the door for Turner/Devcon to build the project in four separate parts, as if building four different structures. SAP Tower was built just like an office building. The eastern sideline, and the north and south end zones, rose up alongside the suite tower, all built from the ground at the same time. Once the tower was up, Levi's Stadium had its signature look. If you cast your eye toward 4900 Marie P. DeBartolo Way from anywhere near the stadium, the snow-white edifice with the red Levi's "batwing" stakes the stadium's place.

The rest of the stadium fell into line, piece by piece. The installation of a "spider web of access points," as Marathe calls them, was designed by former Facebook employees to make Levi's Stadium the most Wi-Fi–friendly stadium ever. Says Dan Williams, vice president of technology, "Our goal was to provide fans solid connectivity so they could be connected while at the game. Our unique Wi-Fi network design enables this as we associate every 100 seats to a specific Wi-Fi access point within the bowl, which provides great coverage and capacity for modern devices. Couple our Wi-Fi network with our cellular distributed antenna system and we feel we accomplished exactly what we set out to do with connectivity at the stadium." The team also likes to emphasize, proudly, the building's environmentally friendly features, particularly the 20,000 square feet of solar panels, which make Levi's Stadium net neutral on the grid; the week it opened, the stadium was bestowed with a LEED (Leadership in Energy & Environmental Design, a green building certification program that recognizes best-in-class building strategies and

The SAP Tower is the architectural masterstroke of Levi's Stadium, allowing for maximum seating in the lower bowl and eliminating the "nosebleed" section entirely.

THESE PAGES: Overhead, side, and cross-sectional renderings of SAP Tower

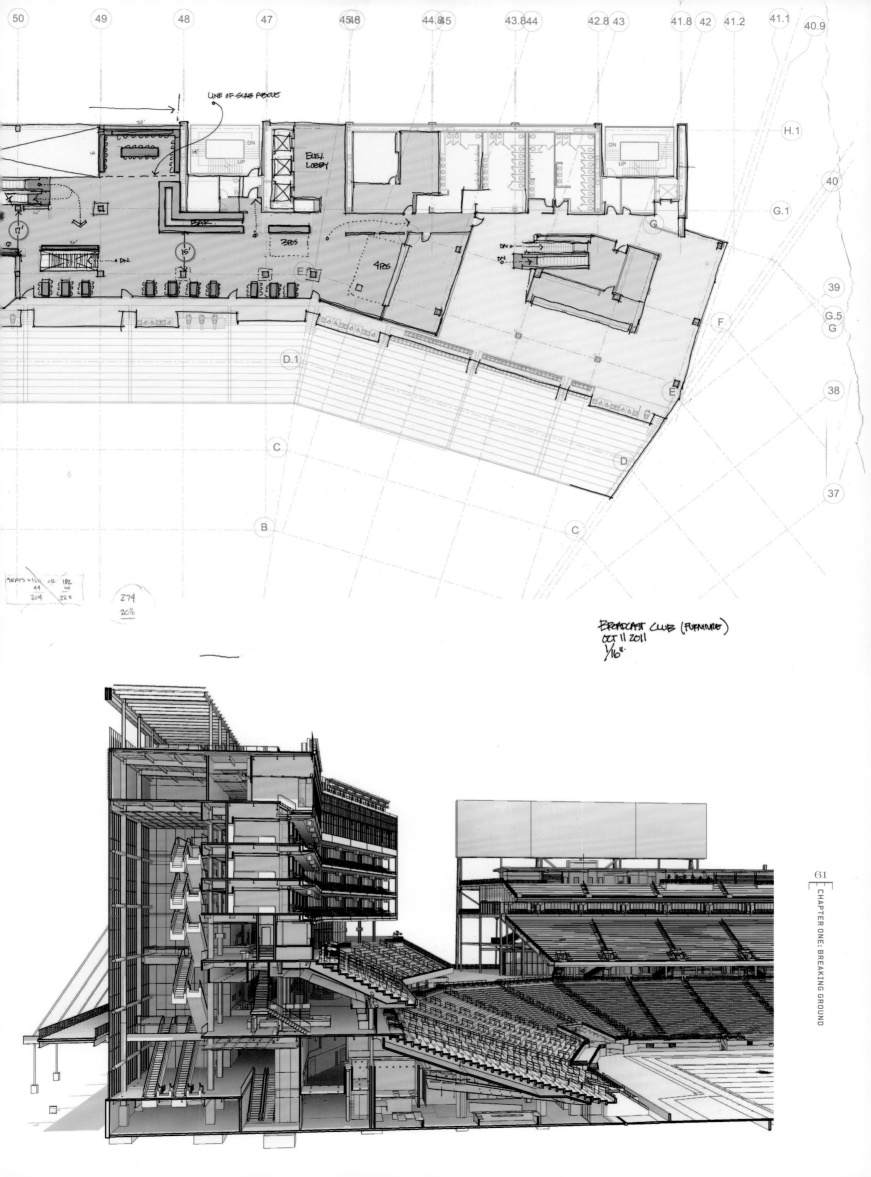

BROADCAST CLUB (FURNITURE)
OCT 11 2011
1/16"

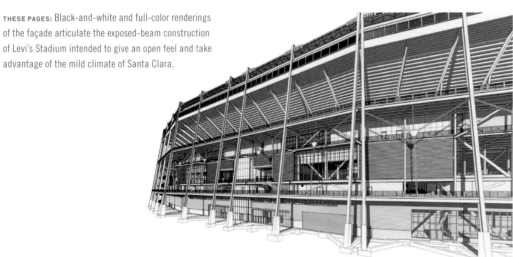

practices) gold certification by the U.S. Green Building Council. The 63-foot-wide concourses—two of them circling the stadium, including an outside "express lane" ringing the field—make for pedestrian flow that Candlestick, with its 19-foot-wide concourses, could never have hoped for.

Jed York and Paraag Marathe boast that Levi's Stadium challenges the status quo and fulfills the team's desire to make not just the newest stadium, but the smartest stadium. In addition to calling it "the physical manifestation of Silicon Valley," Marathe likes the open-air feel of Levi's Stadium, and he points to the exposed beams of white steel and the views of rolling hills nearby. "It's like a South of Market loft," he said. "It feels wide open."

Jack Hill, who has built stadiums all over the country—working alongside former president George W. Bush, politician Ross Perot, and former MLB commissioner Bud Selig along the way—was struck by how Levi's Stadium "reflects the personality of the Bay Area," especially in its environmental standards. "It's amazing to see the structure," he said. "Architects like to say, 'Celebrate the structure.'"

Jonathan Harvey, who had been involved since the DeBartolo days of the late 1990s, assessed the 1.8-million-square-foot stadium, which is more than twice the size of Candlestick Park. "We were challenged throughout to make this building representative of the culture of the region," Harvey said. "Food and wine is important to the Yorks, so there was a heavy emphasis on that culture. But we're also in the heart of Silicon Valley, so the stadium has to be at the forefront of technology.

"It's a response to the region. That's why there's no skin on the building. It's very pure and elegant. It takes advantage of the mild climate. It's an expression of the climate of the region."

Most importantly, though, Harvey explained, this is the 49ers vision made real. "We're designing their house," he said. "This is how the 49ers want to live, and where they want to play football, and how they want their fans to experience football."

Replete with Michael Mina's restaurant . . . the opulent gastronomy of the club areas . . . press box elevators that work . . . a Super Bowl on its way in year two of the stadium . . . the 49ers have found their new home, which is of the Bay Area as much as in it. The 49ers legacy, started nearly seven decades earlier in a different era in the country's history in so many ways, has found its twenty-first-century home.

> "It's a response to the region. That's why there's no skin on the building. It's very pure and elegant. It takes advantage of the mild climate. It's an expression of the climate of the region."

PAGES 64–65: Wide-angle view of Levi's Stadium captured from the NRG Solar Terrace of the SAP Tower

The oldest professional sports franchise born in California didn't always play its football in a gleaming, twenty-first-century temple of modernity.

In fact, the 49ers made their first tackle, completed their first pass, and ran their first touchdown in a simple municipal stadium in the southeast corner of Golden Gate Park, where seagulls swooped from out of the fog, grass faded as the season wore on, and the team charged onto the field from a spartan locker room they shared with local high school football teams.

Kezar Stadium was many things—historic, lacking in amenities, atmospheric, uncomfortable—but most of all, it was the franchise's first home. Like most homes, it was intimate. Sometimes too much so.

"They talk about the 'friendly confines' of Wrigley Field," broadcaster Lon Simmons told NFL Films. "Well, Kezar Stadium wasn't so friendly, but the confines were very close. You could almost touch the players, see their expressions."

PAGES 66–67: 49ers vs. Browns, Kezar Stadium, September 7, 1958

TOP: 49er Bill Wilson receives a fifteen-yard Tittle pass vs. the Colts, December 8, 1957

LEFT AND OPPOSITE: Program covers from the Kezar era

Forty Niners

FORTY NINERS vs. BUFFALO BISONS
NOVEMBER 2, 1946

TOP: The Million Dollar Backfield from left to right: Hugh McElhenny, Joe Perry, Y. A. Tittle, and John Henry Johnson

ABOVE: From left to right: Frankie Albert, Buddy Young, Bob St. Clair, Len Eshmont (81) and Sam Cathcart (83)

On September 8, 1946, the San Francisco 49ers—owned by San Francisco native Tony Morabito, a St. Ignatius and Santa Clara graduate who made his money in the lumber carrier business—lost to the New York Yankees, 21–7, in the first regular-season pro football game ever at Kezar Stadium. Both teams were part of the newly created and short-lived All-America Football Conference (AAFC).

San Francisco sports, ruled up until then by the Seals of baseball's Pacific Coast League, changed forever.

The 49ers played at Kezar from the 1946 through the 1970 seasons, joining the NFL along the way, with many names from those early 49ers teams are enshrined in memory: local stars Frankie Albert, Norm Standlee, and Bruno Banducci of Stanford on that first 49ers team; Hall-of-Famers Y. A. Tittle, Hugh McElhenny, Joe "The Jet" Perry, and John Henry Johnson, who made up the famed "Million Dollar Backfield" in the 1950s; Hall-of-Famers Jimmy Johnson and Dave Wilcox, who guided a ferocious defense to the 1970 NFC Championship game; and quarterback John Brodie, an Oakland kid who

FULLBACK
JOE PERRY

Nicknamed "The Jet" for his quick bursts, Perry was, at the time of his retirement, the 49ers all-time leading rusher (9,723 yards) and second only to Jim Brown in NFL history. Inducted into Canton in 1969, the fullback was the first in NFL history to gain 1,000 yards in two consecutive seasons. Perry joined the 49ers straight from Compton Junior College, where he was teammates with Hugh McElhenny. The 49ers were still members of the All-America Football Conference. Perry, McElhenny, Y. A. Tittle, and John Henry Johnson would form the "Million Dollar Backfield." His No. 34 is retired by the 49ers.

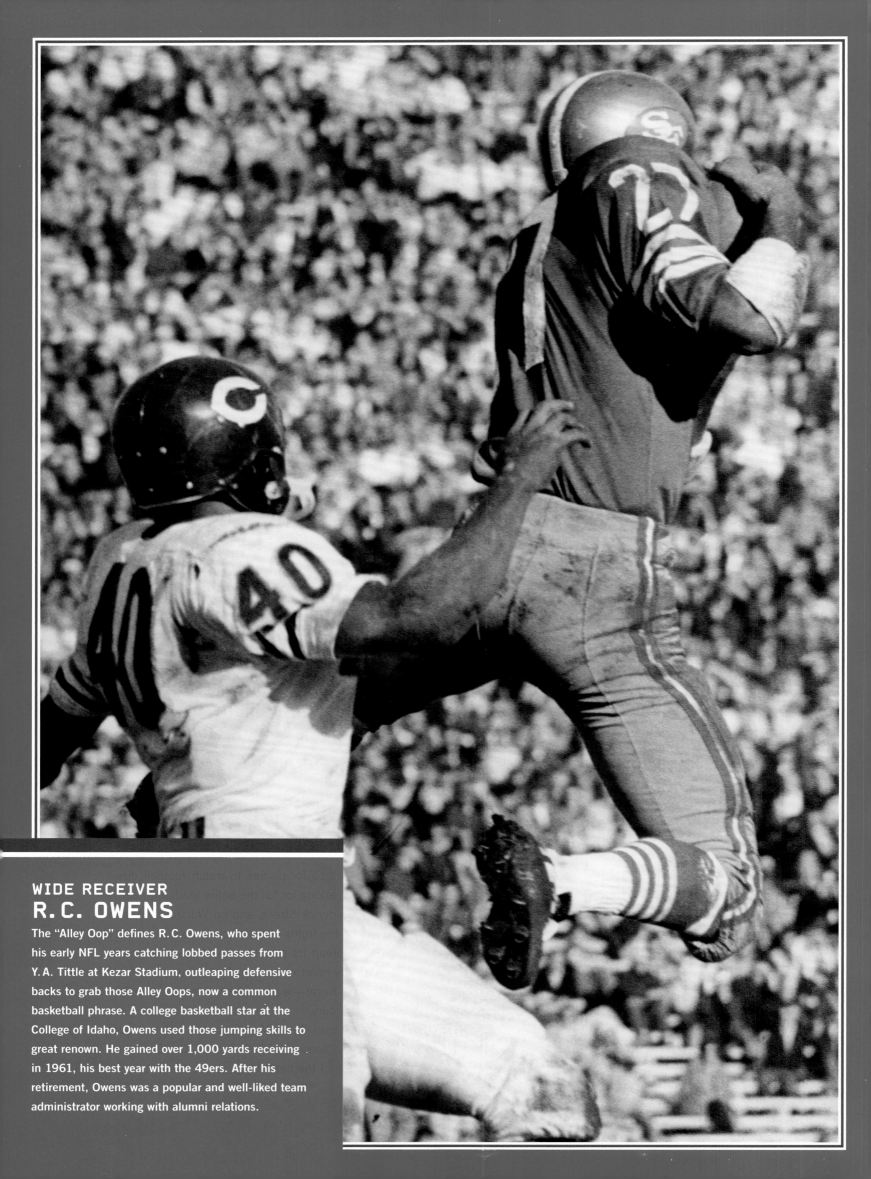

WIDE RECEIVER
R.C. OWENS

The "Alley Oop" defines R.C. Owens, who spent his early NFL years catching lobbed passes from Y. A. Tittle at Kezar Stadium, outleaping defensive backs to grab those Alley Oops, now a common basketball phrase. A college basketball star at the College of Idaho, Owens used those jumping skills to great renown. He gained over 1,000 yards receiving in 1961, his best year with the 49ers. After his retirement, Owens was a popular and well-liked team administrator working with alumni relations.

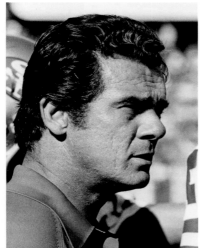

TOP: Coach Dick Nolan, 1973

MIDDLE: Coach Frankie Albert (seated) and Lou Spadia, circa 1957

ABOVE: Coach Buck Shaw, 1949

TOP RIGHT: Quarterback George Mira vs. Packers, October 9, 1966

PAGES 74–75: Left to right: Joe Perry (34), Lou Palatella (68), and Bruce Bosley (77) vs. Colts

made good at Stanford. Brodie was a first-round draft pick in 1957 who wore red and gold all the way through the move to Candlestick Park in 1971.

There was Bob St. Clair, the Hall-of-Famer who played his Poly High football at Kezar, his USF college football at Kezar, and his NFL football at Kezar, earning the right to have the Kezar field named after him; there was R. C. Owens skying for a Tittle pass they called the "Alley Oop"; and there was future San Diego Chargers Hall-of-Famer Dan Fouts watching his father, Bob, call 49ers games on the radio while playing his St. Ignatius football at Kezar.

There was future 49ers Super Bowl coach George Seifert serving as an usher at Kezar in his Poly High days of the 1950s; coach Buck Shaw from Santa Clara taking the first team onto the field in 1946; and coach Dick Nolan taking the team to its first-ever championship game in 1970—the last 49ers game at Kezar before the move to Candlestick Park.

For twenty-four years, the players changed, but Kezar stayed the same, a place ingrained in the city's fabric, with residential apartment buildings so close that fans packed onto rooftops for parties to watch football down below on Sundays. With only a tiny parking lot for the entire stadium, nearby residents on Stanyan Street and Frederick Street, and on Willard, Carl, and Arguello, rented out their garages or the fronts of their houses to make money on parking. Before the Bay Area spread its population wide over the nine-county region, Kezar beat at the very heart of the San Francisco sports fan's mind. The mere name of the place—Kezar—is packed with memories for San Franciscans of the mid-twentieth century.

"In some ways, it was awful," said Gene Washington, a wide receiver who played at Kezar in its final two seasons, 1969 and 1970. "But when you think back and be nostalgic, one of the best things about it was it was a neighborhood stadium."

QUARTERBACK
JOHN BRODIE

The face of the 49ers from Kezar to Candlestick, the quarterback was a Bay Area product all the way through: high school at Oakland Tech, college at Stanford, and then a franchise-record seventeen years with the 49ers. Drafted in the first round in 1957, Brodie was NFL MVP in 1970 and took the 49ers to back-to-back NFC Championship games. By the time he retired, Brodie had amassed the third most passing yards in NFL history. He is second alltime in team history with 31,548 passing yards and third with 214 TD passes. His jersey No. 12 is retired by the team.

NFL football in a place like Kezar is unthinkable in today's world, where the stadium experience is a wonder for the senses. At Levi's Stadium, the 49ers and SCSA have created a fan experience replete with stellar sightlines, the most comfortable seats, and instant access to technology. They've curated the finest food options, a museum, and an art gallery. They've connected the stadium to football fans throughout the Bay Area via multiple modes of public transportation; and they've fashioned, from the ground up, the most environmentally friendly stadium ever built.

At Kezar, the wooden bench seating allowed 16 inches per backside. Parking was virtually nonexistent. Of the nearly sixty thousand seats, only eighteen thousand were between the end zones, making for atrocious sightlines by today's standards. If you wanted a hot dog, it often had to be passed by a dozen fans from the vendor down the wooden bench before it reached you. The only nod to stadium improvement during the 49ers twenty-four-year tenure was the installation of a wire cage over the players' tunnel—to prevent objects thrown by inebriated and salty fans from smashing on players' heads.

One story goes that, after a game between the 49ers and the Baltimore Colts, opposing quarterbacks John Brodie and Johnny Unitas were walking off the field together. The Colts' Johnny U. said to Brodie: "Take your helmet off, John. The game's over." To which Brodie reportedly said: "Wait a minute, and you'll see why I have my helmet on."

Sure enough, bottles and cans soon rained down on Brodie. Linebacker Ed Beard, who witnessed the exchange, explained: "We had some very, very avid football fans at that point, in a stadium where they were able to show what they thought."

ABOVE: Fans at Kezar Stadium

What was Kezar like? Thinking back on his time as the 49ers quarterback, from 1951 to 1960, the great Yelberton Abraham (Y. A.) Tittle said: "It was like I had seen in the movies about the Roman Colosseum. The slaves coming out to be fed to the lions and people up there cheering.

"If you're losing in Kezar Stadium and coming out that long tunnel, you feel like you're going out to the Roman Colosseum and they're going to feed you to the lions." But Tittle wasn't without admiration for the place, adding: "It was a great stadium, and a great thrill to play there."

It was, after all, home for the first generation of San Francisco 49ers players and fans. For generations-deep San Franciscans, it was even more than that. It was the city's showcase stadium, a nearly sixty-thousand-seat arena finished in 1925 at the cost of $300,000.

The first $100,000 came from the estate of Mary Kezar, who left the money with a request to build a memorial to her family, pioneer San Francisco residents. The rest of the money came from the city, making Kezar a mostly public-financed stadium.

The stadium wasn't built to house an NFL team. When it opened on May 2, 1925, the National Football League was only three years old. Begun as the American Professional Football Conference in 1920, the conference changed its name to the NFL in 1922. From the 1924 NFL season that preceded Kezar's opening, the only teams you'd recognize today are the Green Bay Packers and Chicago Bears. The 1924 defending champion Cleveland Bulldogs are no longer around, nor are their prime competitor, the Frankfort Yellow Jackets. The 1925 NFL season saw the birth of the New York Giants, who, of course, in decades to come, would play the 49ers in many important playoff games.

Kezar was built as a track stadium, and its first official event was to host the Olympic legend Paavo "The Flying Finn" Nurmi, the astounding distance runner who won nine Olympic gold medals—including two on one day at the 1924 London Games, when he won both the 1,500 meters and 5,000 meters within two hours of each other. Nurmi opened Kezar with a race against his fellow countryman Ville Ritola.

"If you're losing in Kezar Stadium and coming out that long tunnel, you feel like you're going out to the Roman Colosseum and they're going to feed you to the lions."

TOP: 49ers bench from left to right: Hal Schoener, Jim Power, Johnny Strzykalski, Alyn Beals, Lowell Wagner, and Ziggy Zamlynski (kneeling)

PAGES 82–83: 49ers Hugh McElhenny (39) and Bruce Bosley (77) vs. Chicago Bears' Charley Sumner (26), Joe Fortunato (31), and Doug Atkins (81), October 26, 1958

High school football thrived at Kezar in the pre-49ers years. As many as fifty thousand fans reportedly crammed into Kezar to see Lowell High play Poly High—which sat adjacent to Kezar—in 1928. Kezar then hosted many events for San Franciscans to enjoy— auto racing, rugby, motorcycle racing, lacrosse, and even a celebrated visit from Australia's national cricket team in 1932.

Then in 1946, the San Francisco 49ers—named for the prospectors who rushed to the Golden State in 1849—took the field. A city fell in love.

Generations of fans tell of memories of catching the 71 Noriega or 72 Sunset Muni bus to Kezar to watch the Niners. Some would take the Muni to Irving Street, hop out, buy Christopher Milk at a local grocery store, and then walk down to the stadium.

Christopher Milk—the dairy owned by then San Francisco mayor George Christopher (and today named Berkeley Farms)—appealed to young 49ers fans with a unique promotion. The milk cartons featured free tickets to Kezar for "Junior 49ers," as long as you bought the milk and tore out the ticket from the back of the wax carton. The "Christopher Milk Section" was a stalwart feature of Kezar, even if fans at halftime would, as native San Franciscan Rodney McDonough recounted, "jump over the fence with the guards chasing us to go move into good seats."

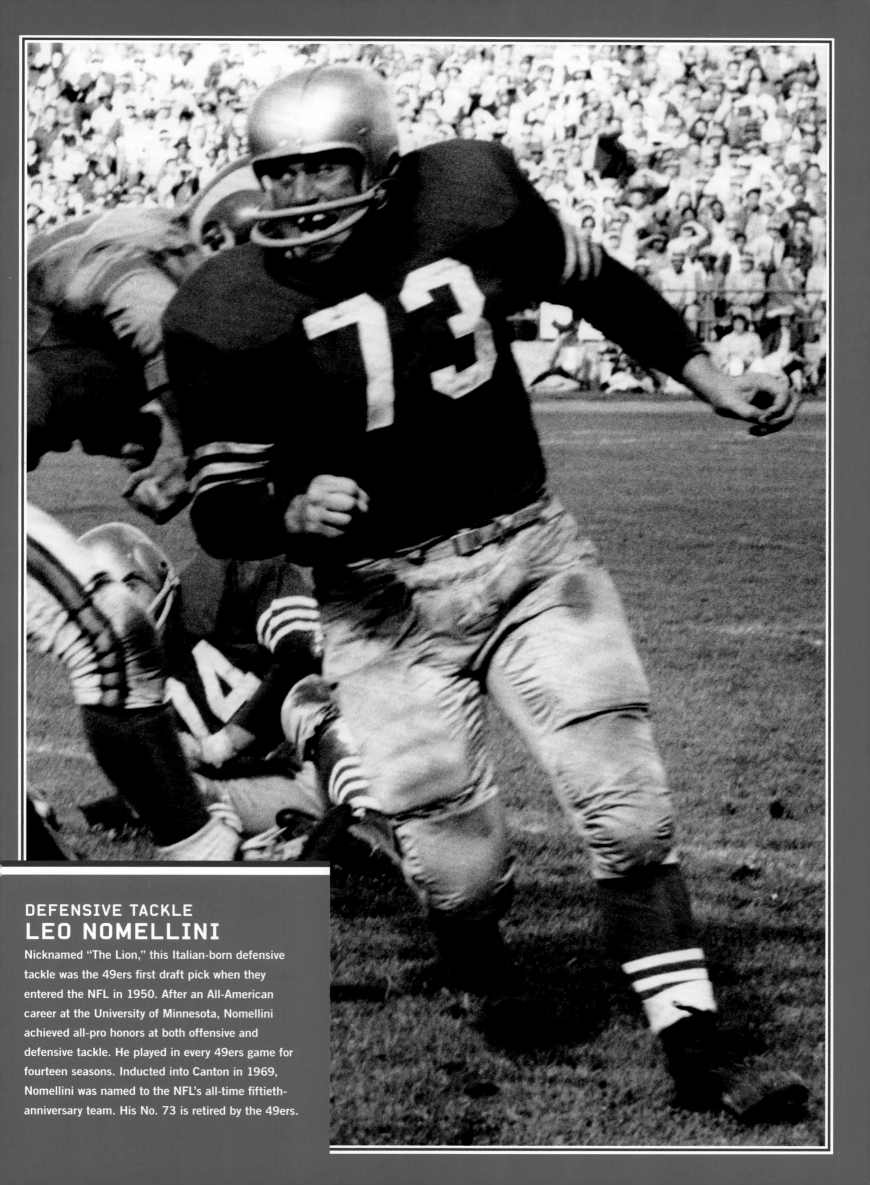

DEFENSIVE TACKLE
LEO NOMELLINI

Nicknamed "The Lion," this Italian-born defensive tackle was the 49ers first draft pick when they entered the NFL in 1950. After an All-American career at the University of Minnesota, Nomellini achieved all-pro honors at both offensive and defensive tackle. He played in every 49ers game for fourteen seasons. Inducted into Canton in 1969, Nomellini was named to the NFL's all-time fiftieth-anniversary team. His No. 73 is retired by the 49ers.

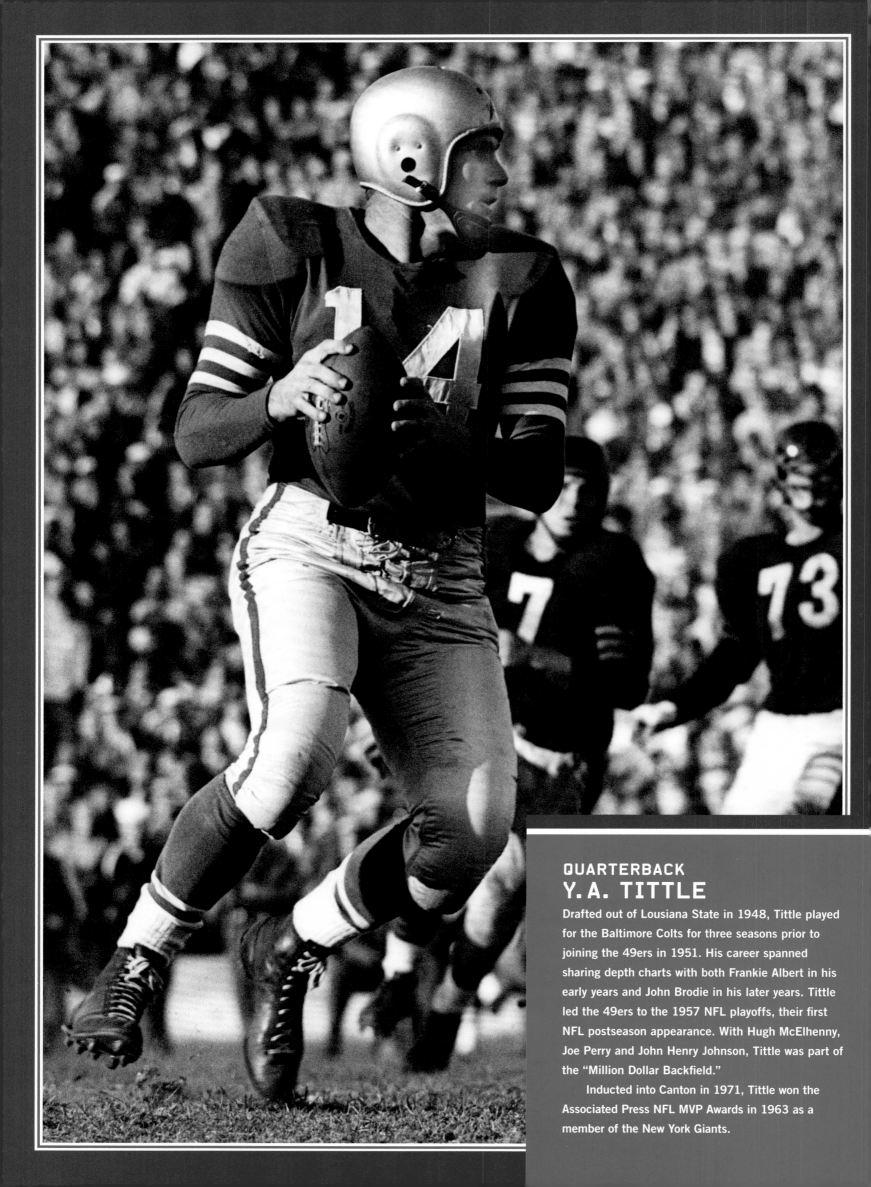

QUARTERBACK
Y. A. TITTLE

Drafted out of Lousiana State in 1948, Tittle played for the Baltimore Colts for three seasons prior to joining the 49ers in 1951. His career spanned sharing depth charts with both Frankie Albert in his early years and John Brodie in his later years. Tittle led the 49ers to the 1957 NFL playoffs, their first NFL postseason appearance. With Hugh McElhenny, Joe Perry and John Henry Johnson, Tittle was part of the "Million Dollar Backfield."

Inducted into Canton in 1971, Tittle won the Associated Press NFL MVP Awards in 1963 as a member of the New York Giants.

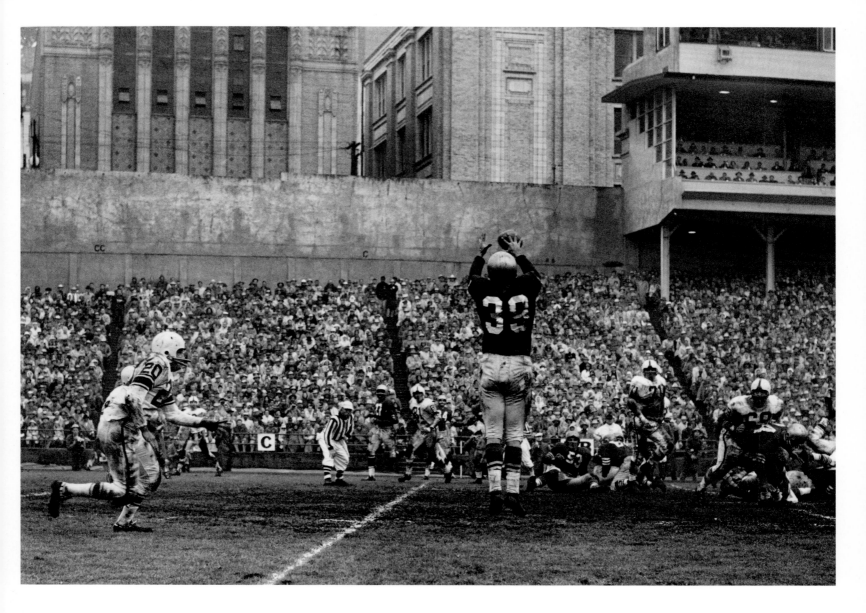

TOP: McElhenny reception on winning drive vs. Green Bay Packers, December 15, 1957

ABOVE: Tittle to R. C. Owens "Alley Oop" vs. Detroit Lions, November 11, 1958

Kezar was a neighborhood stadium, the kind no NFL team could build today, given infrastructure demands and real estate costs. It sat on the western end of the Upper Haight, just blocks from the corner of Haight and Ashbury, which surely made for strange bedfellows when the Summer of Love coincided with the 1967 NFL season.

"Matt Hazeltine and I would drive to Kezar around 10 a.m. after breakfast at the team hotel," said Dave Wilcox, referring to his fellow Pro Bowl linebacker. "We'd drive down Haight Street on Sunday mornings because that was the entrance to Golden Gate Park. It was interesting. I'll put it at that."

Cedrick Hardman, a first-round draft pick defensive end out of North Texas, joined the 49ers in 1970. His rookie season was Kezar's final year, and coming from the Lone Star State to the long-hair capital made an impression.

"You had the hippies. It was during the hippie time," Hardman said. "Woodstock had been the prior summer, and it was an interesting time in America, especially for a country boy coming from Texas."

Or, as longtime 49ers fan Irwin Hurlihy put it: "We used to walk through Golden Gate Park to get to the stadium. There was a big meadow, and you'd smell a lot of strange things coming out of it. And you'd hear flutes, and you'd look up in the trees and there was a hippie, playing some kind of instrument. But it was a beautiful walk, and everything turned out just fine."

Kezar's neighborhood extended south to the hill on Parnassus Avenue, where the UCSF hospital is still perched. From there, the aerial vista looking down on Kezar made the original stadium look like a magical place. Fifth-generation San Franciscan Francine Cunnie was born at UCSF, one of eight

"All those great players," George Seifert said. "But they couldn't quite crack the nut."

BELOW: Fred Morrison of the Chicago Bears punting; Leo Nomellini (42) attempts to block the punt, circa 1950

PAGES 88-89: Harry Gilmer of the Washington Redskins runs through the Kezar fog after taking a pitchout from Jack Scarbath (18), but the fourth quarter effort was not enough to overtake the 49ers at home; September 26, 1954. Final score: Redskins 7, 49ers 41

children in her family. Francine's father and grandfather, sitting with her mother after she had given birth during football season, peered out the glass on a Kezar football Sunday, gazing down like children with noses pressed against a bakery window.

"My mom knew they were just dying to go," she said. "So, being the 49er Faithful she is, and a football mother, she released them. She said: 'Okay, go ahead, you guys, go to the game!' They couldn't get their stuff together soon enough to get down the hill and watch the 49ers play at Kezar Stadium."

What they saw was not exactly championship football. The 49ers enjoyed success as an AAFC team, posting winning records from 1946 to 1949 and making it to the 1949 AAFC Championship game before losing to Otto Graham and the Cleveland Browns, yet their twenty-one NFL seasons at Kezar from 1950 to 1970 resulted in only two playoff appearances. "All those great players," George Seifert said. "But they couldn't quite crack the nut."

The Kezar years, instead, are a collage of players who wore the red and gold and a few moments of glory and football brilliance framed by seagulls, fog, and raucous fans who occasionally heaved those flying objects.

Most notably, the Kezar years included the "Million Dollar Backfield" from 1954 to 1960, which was made up of quarterback Y. A. Tittle and running backs Joe Perry, Hugh McElhenny, and John Henry Johnson (who was traded in 1957). They never won an NFL playoff game together, but they dazzled athletically, and they became the first NFL backfield to have all four members land in Canton's Hall of Fame, enshrined forever.

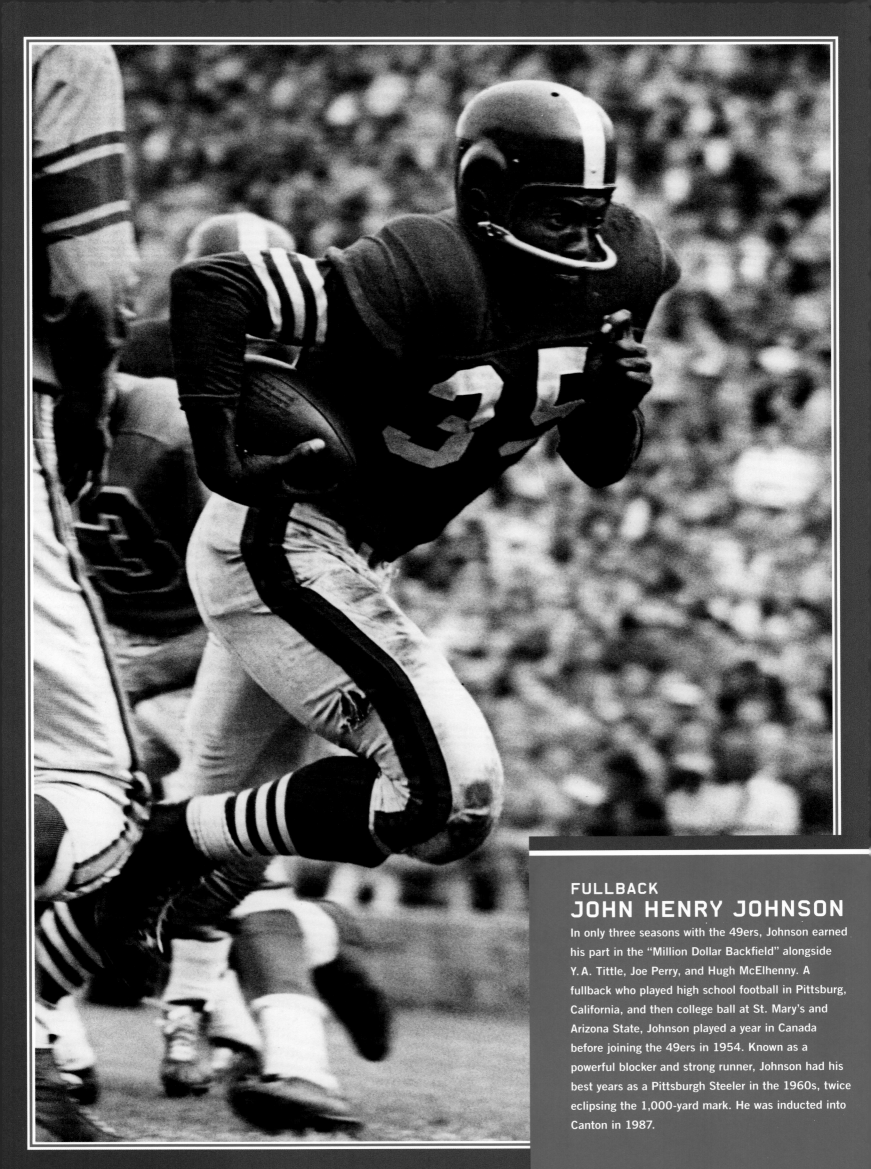

FULLBACK
JOHN HENRY JOHNSON

In only three seasons with the 49ers, Johnson earned his part in the "Million Dollar Backfield" alongside Y. A. Tittle, Joe Perry, and Hugh McElhenny. A fullback who played high school football in Pittsburg, California, and then college ball at St. Mary's and Arizona State, Johnson played a year in Canada before joining the 49ers in 1954. Known as a powerful blocker and strong runner, Johnson had his best years as a Pittsburgh Steeler in the 1960s, twice eclipsing the 1,000-yard mark. He was inducted into Canton in 1987.

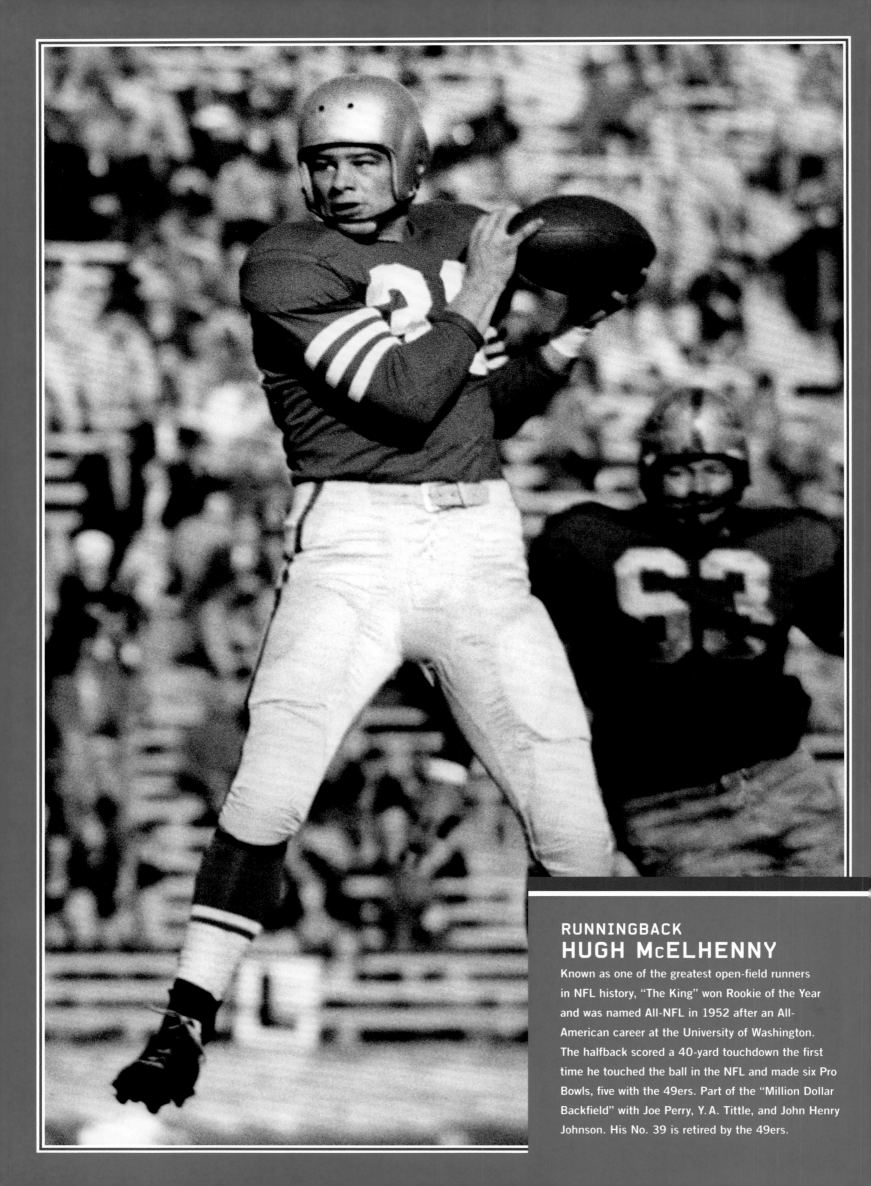

RUNNINGBACK
HUGH McELHENNY

Known as one of the greatest open-field runners in NFL history, "The King" won Rookie of the Year and was named All-NFL in 1952 after an All-American career at the University of Washington. The halfback scored a 40-yard touchdown the first time he touched the ball in the NFL and made six Pro Bowls, five with the 49ers. Part of the "Million Dollar Backfield" with Joe Perry, Y. A. Tittle, and John Henry Johnson. His No. 39 is retired by the 49ers.

McElhenny was an open-field genius, a dashing, darting, whirling presence whose dazzling style earned him the nickname "The King." Seifert remembers being a teenage fan and waiting to see McElhenny exit the locker room after games, also marveling at the King's style. McElhenny always wore the finest tailored suits. "Spiffy," Seifert said. When he retired after the 1963 season, McElhenny was one of only three players in league history to have amassed over 11,000 all-purpose yards. "The best broken field runner that ever played," Tittle said. "You could hardly touch him."

John Henry Johnson bruised his way to over 6,000 rushing yards, fourth-best in league history when he retired. "He'd get in fights with the defense, and they'd take it out on me," Tittle said, laughing. "If he wasn't a football player, he'd have been a fighter, and never lost a match." At six-foot-two, 210 pounds, Johnson didn't take "no" for an answer.

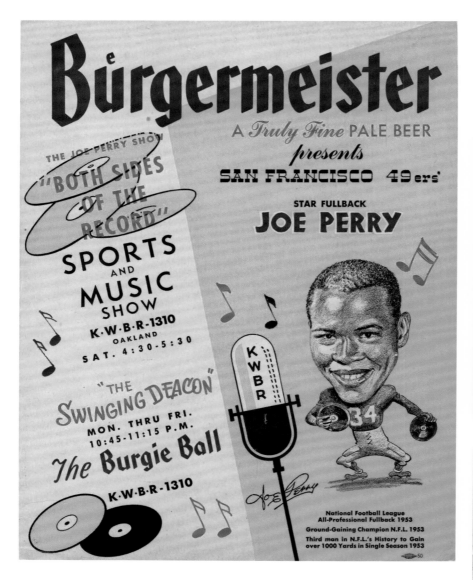

If McElhenny was "The King," Joe Perry was "The Jet," a player whose rushing total was third all-time in NFL annals when he retired. Old footage shows Perry bursting through the line with great speed. Tittle says he was so quick on the ball, "I couldn't even get the ball from center to get to him. He was gone through the hole."

Fans at Kezar also witnessed the creation of the "Alley Oop." Quarterback Y. A. Tittle would loft passes to receiver R. C. Owens, who used his University of Idaho basketball skills to outleap defenders and make the catch. The key to the "Alley Oop," said Tittle, "was that Owens didn't want a spiral. He wanted it to flutter like a duck [to make it] easier to snatch it out of the air. He said he could judge it better if it was wobbling."

Tittle laughed as he remembered. "Here I am, proud of my passing arm, and I've got to throw the ball up in the air for grabs. But R. C. would stand on the outside and swoop in at the last second and pluck it out of the air."

Then there was Jim "Wrong Way" Marshall, the Minnesota Vikings defensive end who recovered a 49ers fumble in an October 25, 1964 game. Somehow, Marshall got turned around and ran the ball . . . the wrong way, all the way into the 49ers end zone for one of the biggest gaffes in NFL history. Marshall ran 66 yards, crossed the goal line untouched, and tossed the ball into the air in celebration as several 49ers linemen caught up to him. Center Bruce Bosley, No. 77, patted Marshall on the shoulder pads, thanking him for the safety and the two points.

ABOVE: Magic Eye breakdown of a Tittle to R. C. Owens "Alley Oop"

PAGES 94–95: Joe Perry on a sixteen yard scoring play vs. Detroit Lions, 1955

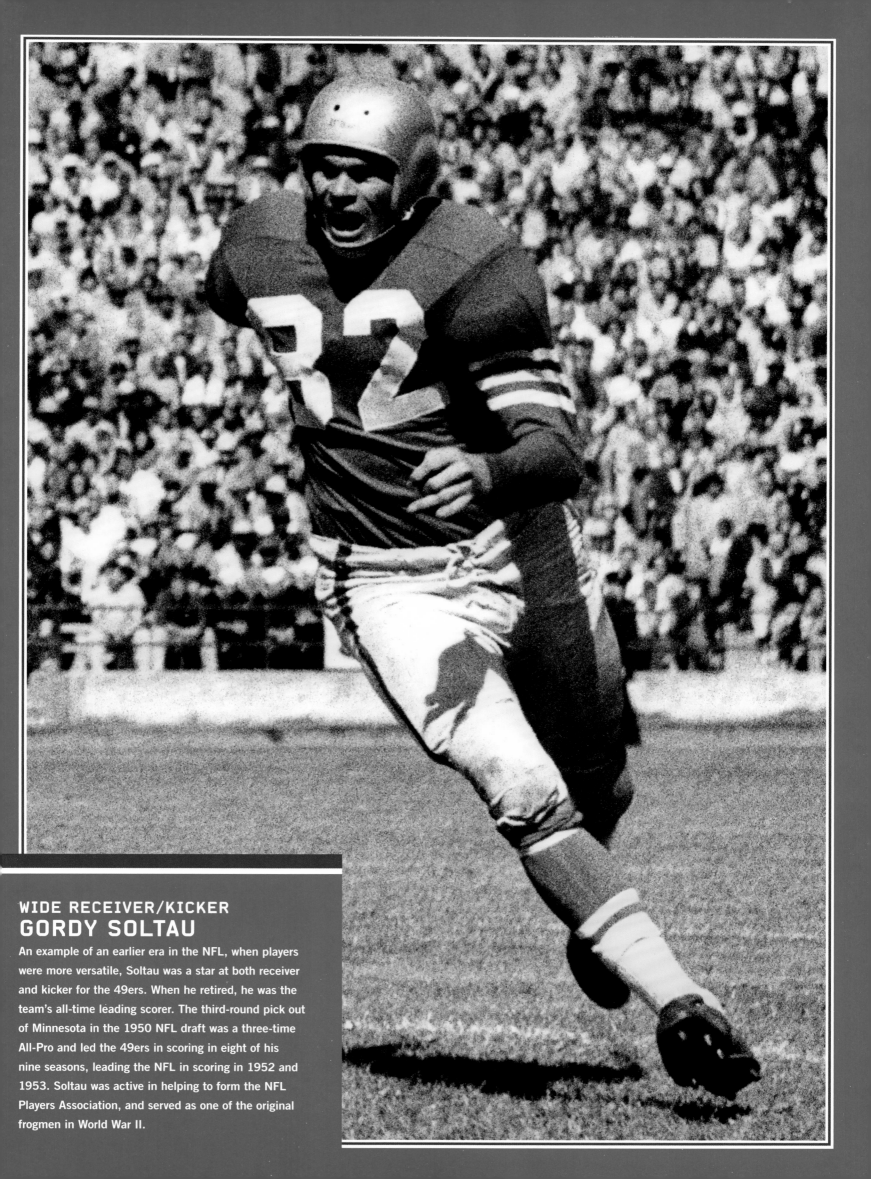

WIDE RECEIVER/KICKER
GORDY SOLTAU

An example of an earlier era in the NFL, when players were more versatile, Soltau was a star at both receiver and kicker for the 49ers. When he retired, he was the team's all-time leading scorer. The third-round pick out of Minnesota in the 1950 NFL draft was a three-time All-Pro and led the 49ers in scoring in eight of his nine seasons, leading the NFL in scoring in 1952 and 1953. Soltau was active in helping to form the NFL Players Association, and served as one of the original frogmen in World War II.

CO-OWNERS
TONY AND VIC MORABITO

Tony Morabito founded San Francisco's first major league professional sports franchise in 1946, naming them for the gold rush miners of 1849. Tony and his brother, Vic Morabito, moved the team from the All-America Football Conference to the NFL in 1950. The brothers from San Francisco prepped at St. Ignatius High and drafted and signed all the big-name players of the 49ers early era. After Tony Morabito's death in 1957, Vic Morabito ran the team until his death in 1964.

> "I do know it rattled the team," Tittle said. "I think we just emotionally decided we were going to win the game for Tony."

"We had guys chasing him," said Dave Wilcox. "And they're going to try to tackle him. And I'm thinking, thank god Marshall can outrun them all, or they would have tackled him short of a safety. So that was classic."

One memorable tragedy occurred during a game on October 27, 1957: 49ers owner Tony Morabito suddenly died of a heart attack at Kezar while watching a 49ers-Bears game. Morabito was only forty-seven. During intermission, Coach Frankie Albert, an original 49ers player, told the team in their no-frills locker room of Morabito's passing. The 49ers were shaken but inspired. Down 17–7 at that point, the team rallied to the win the game, 21–17.

"I do know it rattled the team," Tittle said. "I think we just emotionally decided we were going to win the game for Tony."

The 49ers not only won that game but made the 1957 playoffs. The first NFL playoff game at Kezar Stadium was played on December 22, and the entire city of San Francisco would mourn it for years—the 49ers blew a 24–7 lead and lost to quarterback Tobin Rote and the Detroit Lions, 27–24. Seifert, a seventeen-year-old high schooler at the time, spoke of the "gloom and doom" that hung over the city. Tittle was similarly disconsolate. "I've blanked that out of my mind forever," the quarterback said. "I wiped it out of the memory chart."

TOP: Gordy Soltau kicks the winning field goal vs. Pittsburgh Steelers, 1958

LEFT: Magic Eye breakdown of a comeback touchdown vs. Chicago Bears, October 27, 1957

PAGES 98–99: Kermit Alexander with an interception vs. Philadelphia Eagles, November 20, 1966

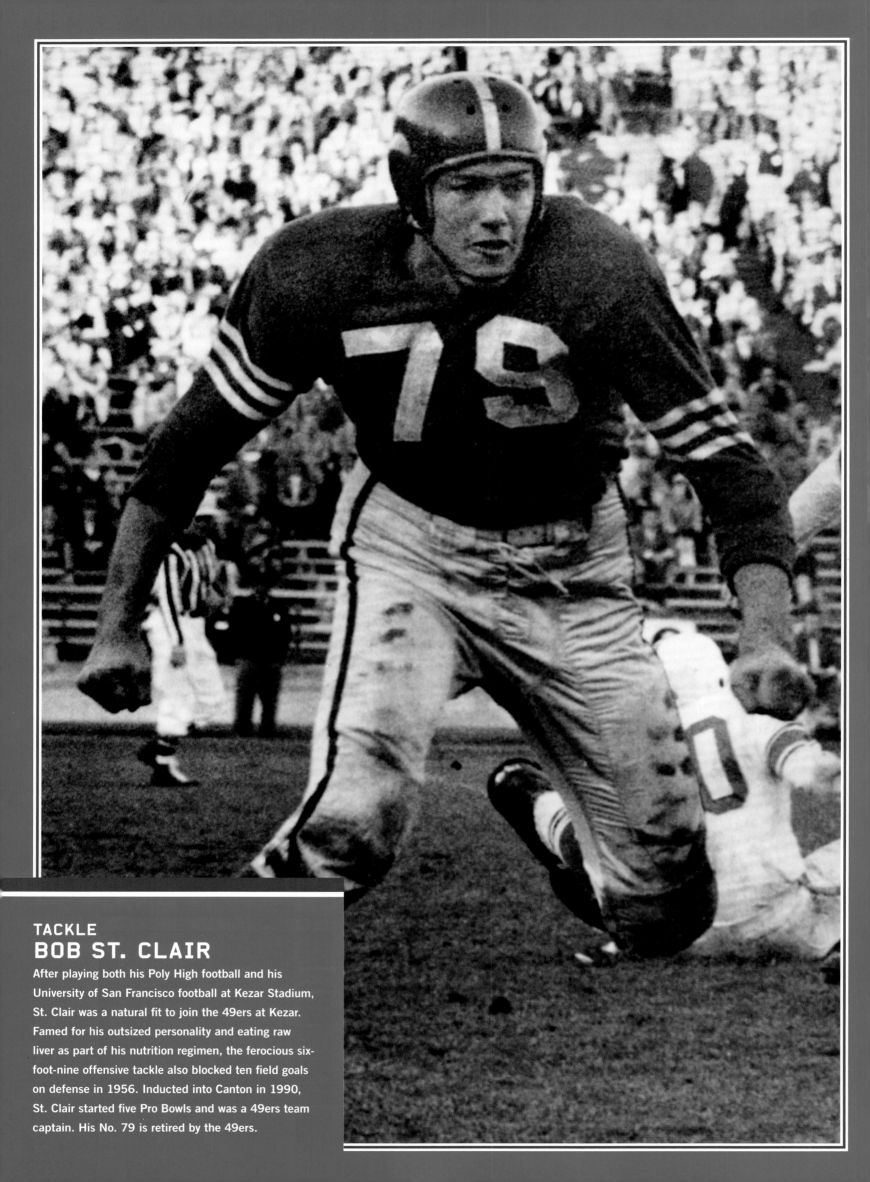

TACKLE
BOB ST. CLAIR
After playing both his Poly High football and his
University of San Francisco football at Kezar Stadium,
St. Clair was a natural fit to join the 49ers at Kezar.
Famed for his outsized personality and eating raw
liver as part of his nutrition regimen, the ferocious six-
foot-nine offensive tackle also blocked ten field goals
on defense in 1956. Inducted into Canton in 1990,
St. Clair started five Pro Bowls and was a 49ers team
captain. His No. 79 is retired by the 49ers.

All the while, Kezar provided more memories. Seifert remembers the Baltimore Colts practicing on the Poly High practice field down near the Golden Gate Park merry-go-round the day before a game, and Hall-of-Famers Johnny Unitas and Raymond Berry sticking around after practice, working on pass routes until near darkness amid the trees of the city's iconic park.

The Kezar years climaxed in 1970 with the best team the 49ers ever fielded at the stadium—the 10–3–1 Niners, who led the NFL in scoring behind MVP quarterback John Brodie, Coach of the Year Dick Nolan (father of future 49ers coach Mike Nolan), and Defensive Rookie of the Year cornerback Bruce Taylor. They won the coldest game in franchise history, to that point, by upsetting the 12-win Vikings in Minnesota, 17–14, on December 27, 1970. The win earned them the January 3, 1971, date at Kezar versus the Dallas Cowboys, the beginning of a decades-long entanglement with the boys in blue. The game enabled the 49ers to close the Kezar era at home in Golden Gate Park. The team was set to move to the modern Candlestick Park for the 1971 season, then already the home of San Francisco Giants baseball for eleven years. Willie Mays, Juan Marichal, and Willie McCovey would see their ballpark enclosed and enlarged to welcome San Francisco's NFL team, but first there was an NFC Championship game to be played in Golden Gate Park.

It did not end well. The Cowboys outlasted the 49ers, 17–10, and punched their ticket to Super Bowl V.

In keeping with Kezar's decades-long reputation as the home of the unabashed and the vocal, some unruly fans went wild, tearing up the wooden seats, even brawling. Thirteen people were treated for cuts and bruises, and twenty-two were arrested in what a San Francisco policeman called a "fandango through the stands. . . . I don't know if it was camaraderie or a disgust with the game that started it."

This was Kezar to the core: raw and unvarnished. It was a place where its overuse from high schools and the NFL wore down the grass as the year lengthened, and some players remember the playing surface as essentially green-painted sand. It was a place where nearly every player remembers the

THESE PAGES: 1957 NFC Playoffs vs. Detroit Lions

afternoon seagulls and their droppings and, of course, that famous wire cage over the tunnel to protect players from flying objects hurled by rabid fans. It was a place where some remember the afternoon fog laying so low a kicked ball might disappear briefly into the mist. It was a place that team general manager Lou Spadia said he couldn't wait to get out of, so they could move to

RIGHT: Cedrick Hardman

OPPOSITE: Coach Frankie Albert, December 7, 1958

PAGES 106-107: Frankie Albert as a player vs. Los Angeles Rams, 1950

gleaming Candlestick, with its mezzanine suites and acres of parking. Kezar's charm had its limits. Fans once complained to team management that their car's hubcaps were stolen by ne'er-do-wells roaming Golden Gate Park. In one instance, during the final season, singer John Davidson rode a horse around the stadium to charge up the crowd prior to singing a rousing rendition of the "Star-Spangled Banner," only to dismount and find Kezar's sound system had crapped out. There would be no national anthem.

And yet, like so many lost ballparks on the American sporting scene, it's memory is wrapped in a heavy cloak of nostalgia. A new, smaller stadium replaced the original Kezar in 1989, but for many longtime San Franciscans and 49ers fans, it's just not the same. Kezar will always be the place—sightlines be damned—where their beloved team was born. "It's where we all grew up," Seifert said. "The roots of the team were established in Kezar."

Cedrick Hardman was a rookie in Kezar's final year, and he remembers happy inconveniences like overenthusiastic fans breaking his car's antenna in the easily-accessible players' parking lot. He also remembers a quieter side to Kezar.

"My fondest memory is Sunday mornings, driving through Golden Gate Park before the park came alive, and it was just so serene," Hardman said. "Coming from Texas and having heard about Kezar and Golden Gate Park and to know how the park had life when it did come alive . . . but on Sunday mornings when I would drive to the stadium, I'd get there early and it was quiet. It was just at peace. And that stuck with me more than anything.

"I had a designated parking spot, and I'd go into the locker room, and my favorite person then, and still is, John Brodie. I'd go by Brodie's locker and he'd drop some of his wisdom on me. And I'd get fired up."

CHAPTER THREE
THE 'STICK

-10   -20   -30   40

The Catch. The Genius. Joe Cool. Jerry, Ronnie, and Steve. Five Super Bowl-winning seasons. Eight NFC Championship games. Seifert and Mooch. T. O. and "The Catch 2," Harbaugh and the khakis. Alex over the Saints. Kap, Gore, and Willis. And let's not forget AstroTurf, tailgates, and more Monday Night Football games than any stadium in NFL history. Candlestick Park, you left your mark.

Even the 49ers final game at Candlestick Park was punctuated by an indelible moment: the "Pick at the 'Stick," in which NaVorro Bowman intercepted a pass and sprinted 89 yards through the night on December 23, 2013, scoring the touchdown that clinched both the final 49ers victory at the 'Stick, a 34–24 win over Atlanta, as well as a playoff berth. Beneath lights secured by creaky stanchions in what had become the NFL's most outdated stadium, the crowd cheered in full-throated exultation. Yet as happy as everyone was with the outcome of that final game, most everyone also agreed: It was time to leave.

Some forty-three years earlier, the team and its fans had felt the same way about the historic but impractical Kezar Stadium. Then, the 49ers were eager for the modern concrete expanses, mezzanine suites, and vast parking lots of Candlestick Park. In 1971, Kezar was the past. Candlestick was the future.

OPPOSITE: Fred Dean and Archie Reese celebrate the 49ers win over the Los Angeles Rams, October 25, 1981

TOP: Last game at Candlestick Park, December 23, 2013

RIGHT: 49ers at Browns, November 11, 1984

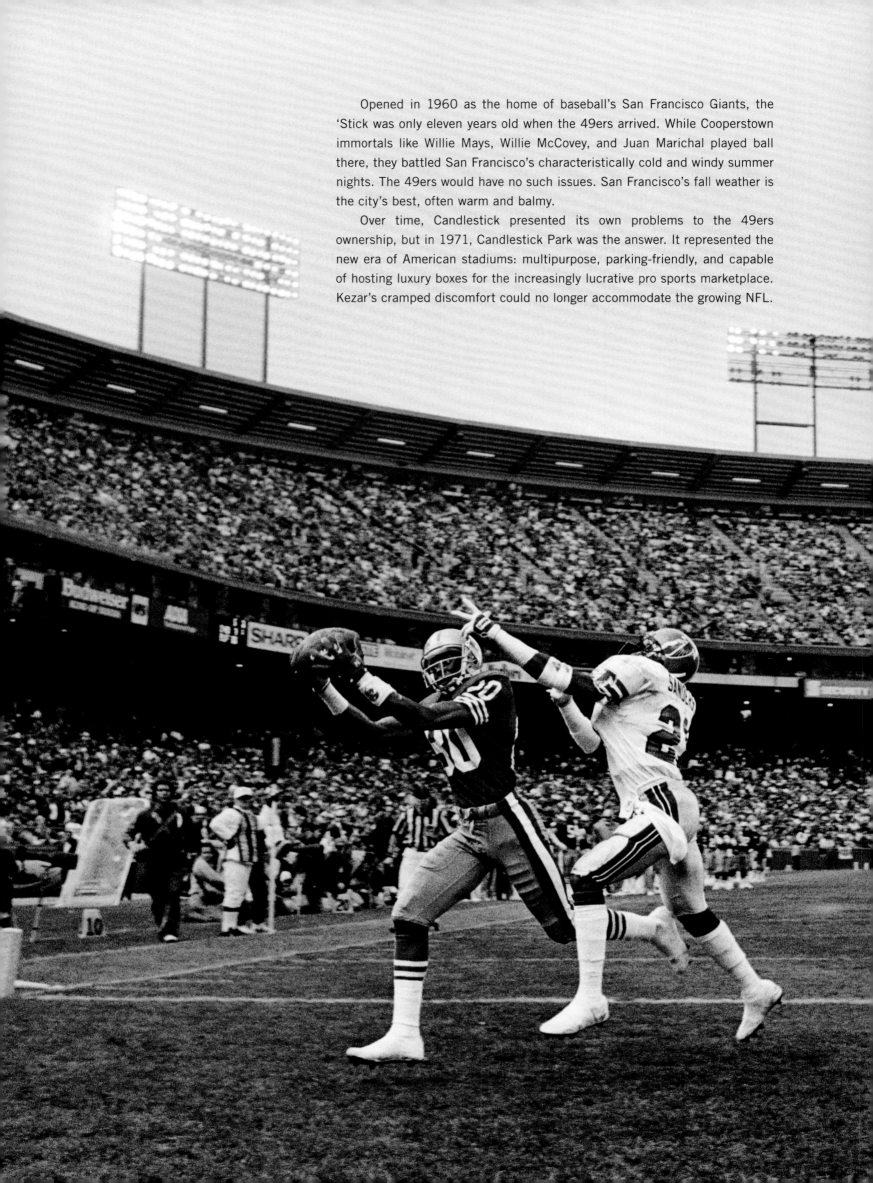

Opened in 1960 as the home of baseball's San Francisco Giants, the 'Stick was only eleven years old when the 49ers arrived. While Cooperstown immortals like Willie Mays, Willie McCovey, and Juan Marichal played ball there, they battled San Francisco's characteristically cold and windy summer nights. The 49ers would have no such issues. San Francisco's fall weather is the city's best, often warm and balmy.

Over time, Candlestick presented its own problems to the 49ers ownership, but in 1971, Candlestick Park was the answer. It represented the new era of American stadiums: multipurpose, parking-friendly, and capable of hosting luxury boxes for the increasingly lucrative pro sports marketplace. Kezar's cramped discomfort could no longer accommodate the growing NFL.

The city of San Francisco paid to enclose Candlestick—which was open-ended behind the baseball outfield fence from 1960 to 1971—to accommodate large NFL crowds, increasing the seating capacity to 61,185. The enclosure made for an oblong shape that some thought resembled a spaceship parked just off Highway 101 near the San Francisco/Brisbane border. In 1971, the place looked futuristic. There was just one problem: When the 49ers got to their new home, they weren't playing on grass.

As bad as Kezar's sometimes inconsistent turf could be, at least it was real, what Mother Nature meant football to be played on. The 49ers, instead, played their first eight seasons at the 'Stick on the scourge of the 1970s—artificial turf. Even worse, the field was marred by "sliding pits," or open swaths of infield dirt from the baseball basepaths. "We called it Candlestone," said Cedrick Hardman, defensive end for the 49ers from 1970 to 1979. "It was a hard turf."

THESE PAGES: Jerry Rice touchdown reception vs. the Atlanta Falcons with Deion Sanders defending

Bill Sandifer, defensive lineman with the 49ers from 1974 to 1976, corroborated the experience: "What a great parking lot to play on. . . . The turf must have been a quarter-inch long, just laid on concrete, I believe. The seams in the field—you felt everything." So much for modern living.

In fact, despite the promise of a new era, Candlestick gave the 49ers precious few good memories in its first decade housing the team. Despite playoff appearances in each of the team's first two years at Candlestick— Dick Nolan's team beat the Redskins in the 1971 divisional playoffs, the first Candlestick playoff win of what would become the team's twenty playoff wins over forty-three seasons—the team's last playoff game of the Nolan Era was the infamous December 23, 1972, divisional loss to Dallas.

ABOVE: Larry Schreiber vs. Los Angeles Rams, September 28, 1975

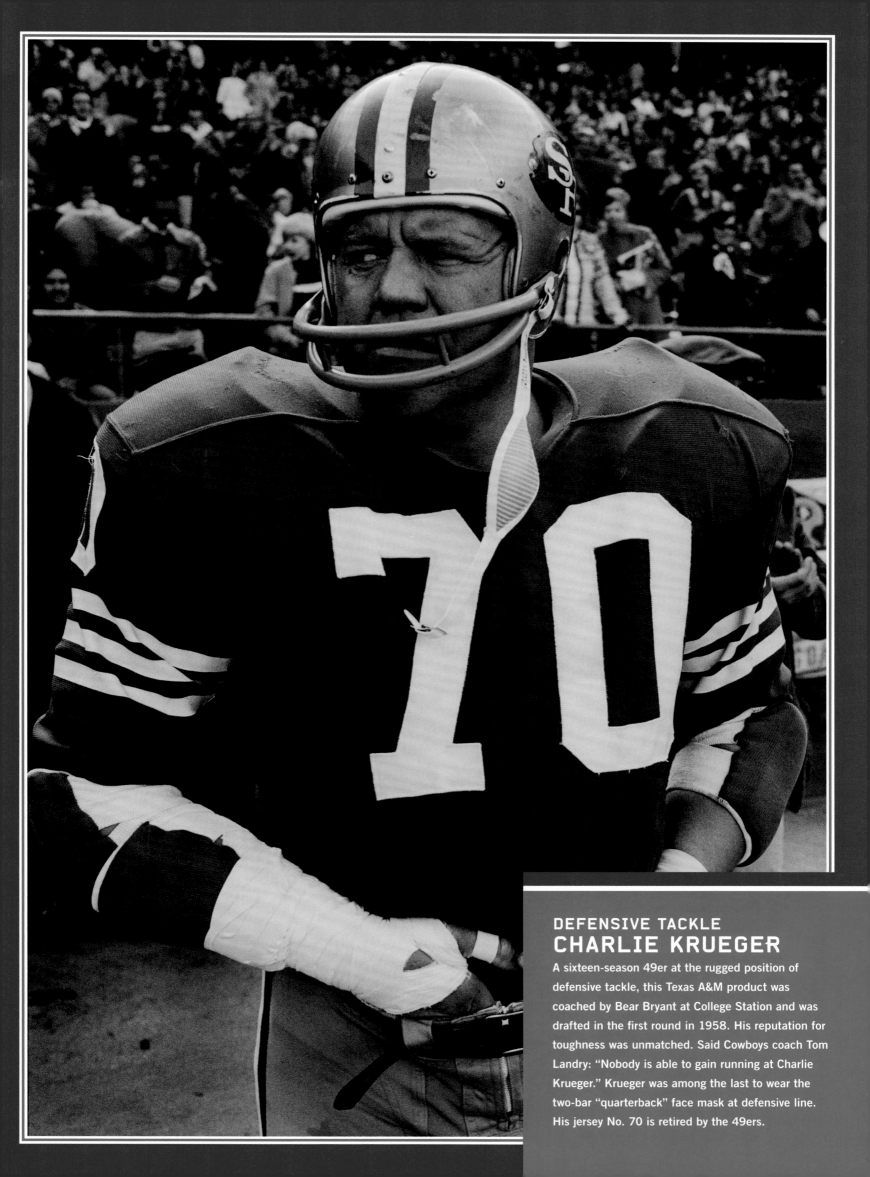

DEFENSIVE TACKLE
CHARLIE KRUEGER

A sixteen-season 49er at the rugged position of defensive tackle, this Texas A&M product was coached by Bear Bryant at College Station and was drafted in the first round in 1958. His reputation for toughness was unmatched. Said Cowboys coach Tom Landry: "Nobody is able to gain running at Charlie Krueger." Krueger was among the last to wear the two-bar "quarterback" face mask at defensive line. His jersey No. 70 is retired by the 49ers.

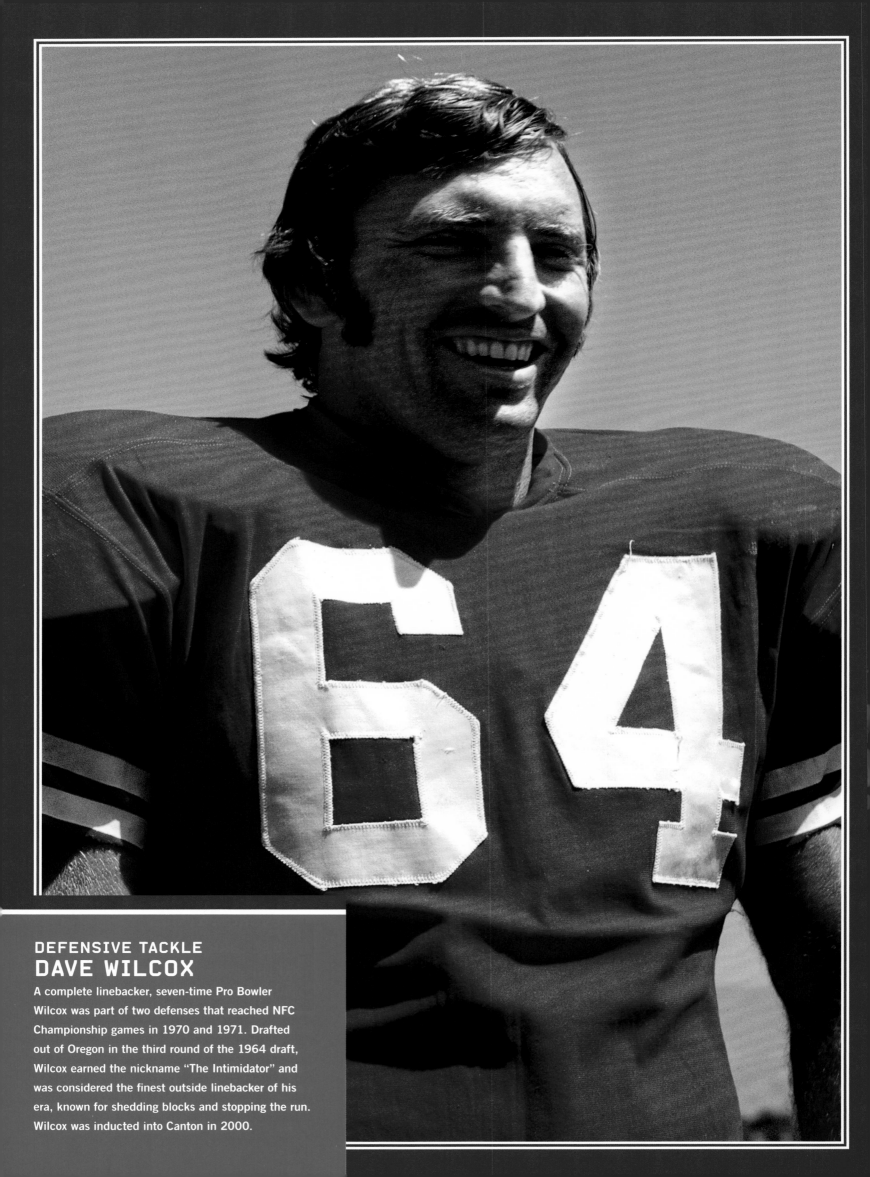

DEFENSIVE TACKLE
DAVE WILCOX

A complete linebacker, seven-time Pro Bowler Wilcox was part of two defenses that reached NFC Championship games in 1970 and 1971. Drafted out of Oregon in the third round of the 1964 draft, Wilcox earned the nickname "The Intimidator" and was considered the finest outside linebacker of his era, known for shedding blocks and stopping the run. Wilcox was inducted into Canton in 2000.

The 49ers blew a 28–13 lead for a 30–28 loss to the Cowboys, which was capped when 49er Preston Riley fumbled an onsides kick, and Dallas scored 17 unanswered points in the fourth quarter for the win. The game spurred memories of the 49ers blown playoff game in 1957 against Detroit at Kezar. The 49ers, it seemed, couldn't win the big one. Adding to the pain, the now-rival Cowboys had punched the ticket home for the 49ers for three straight seasons, from 1970 to 1972. The 49ers, and Candlestick, would garner revenge. It would just take a few years.

Those early Candlestick years in the 1970s were tough ones for a team that had been seeking its first championship since its birth in 1946. After John Brodie retired in 1973, the losses piled up through the rest of the 1970s. No franchise quarterback was found. Remember Tom Owen? Joe Reed? Jim Plunkett (that is, before his Super Bowl glory in Oakland)? Scott Bull? Steve DeBerg? Remember coaches Ken Meyer and Pete McCulley? They all failed to get the 49ers to the postseason.

Despite Pro Bowl play from defensive linemen like Cedrick Hardman and Cleveland Elam and from running back Delvin Williams, attendance was down. Sample attendance figures at Candlestick from the mid-1970s include games like a December 1975 loss to the New York Giants when 33,939 Faithful attended, a September 1976 home-opening loss to Chicago that only drew 44,158, and a December 1978 game against Tampa Bay that drew just 30,931—less than half of Candlestick's capacity. At least the 49ers won that 1978 barnburner against the Buccaneers, 6–3. It helped burnish their 2–14 season.

> The now-rival Cowboys had punched the ticket home for the 49ers for three straight seasons, from 1970 to 1972. The 49ers, and Candlestick, would garner revenge. It would just take a few years.

TOP: Dwight Clark in the game that would begin a 49ers dynasty; NFC Championship vs. Dallas Cowboys, January 10, 1982

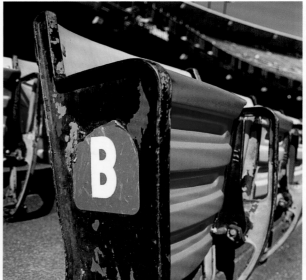

ABOVE: William "Bubba" Paris, pregame taping, November 11, 1985

ABOVE RIGHT: Detail of seat from Candlestick

In that first decade, the characteristic features of Candlestick Park as a football venue led to ingrained routines for 49ers fans on fall Sundays. The rollaway bleachers on the east side of the stadium were the sunniest and the best—a fleet of orange seats from goal line to goal line, so different from the poor sightlines of Kezar. The 49ers players and coaches roamed the west sideline, where afternoon shade kept the sun out of their eyes. When the Faithful were particularly peppy, they would trade chants of "GO! NINERS!" from the east side of the stadium to the west.

Muni ran a Ballpark Express bus that shepherded fans—some in the familiar gold satin jackets with the red-and-white "SF" logo on the left breast and "Forty Niners" in bold on the back—to Candlestick, dropping them off in front of Gate B at the crest of a hill up from the main parking lot.

And the same way Christopher Milk provided childhood memories for kids in the 1950s and 1960s at Kezar, Berkeley Farms and its "Junior 49er Minor Club" granted local kids in the 1970s seats in the southeastern end zone, above a yellow banner proclaiming the section. The seats were free but still exacted a price: the rollaway bleachers on the east side, where the Berkeley Farms club sat, had partially obscured sightlines. That didn't matter much to kids taking in their first 49ers game, though.

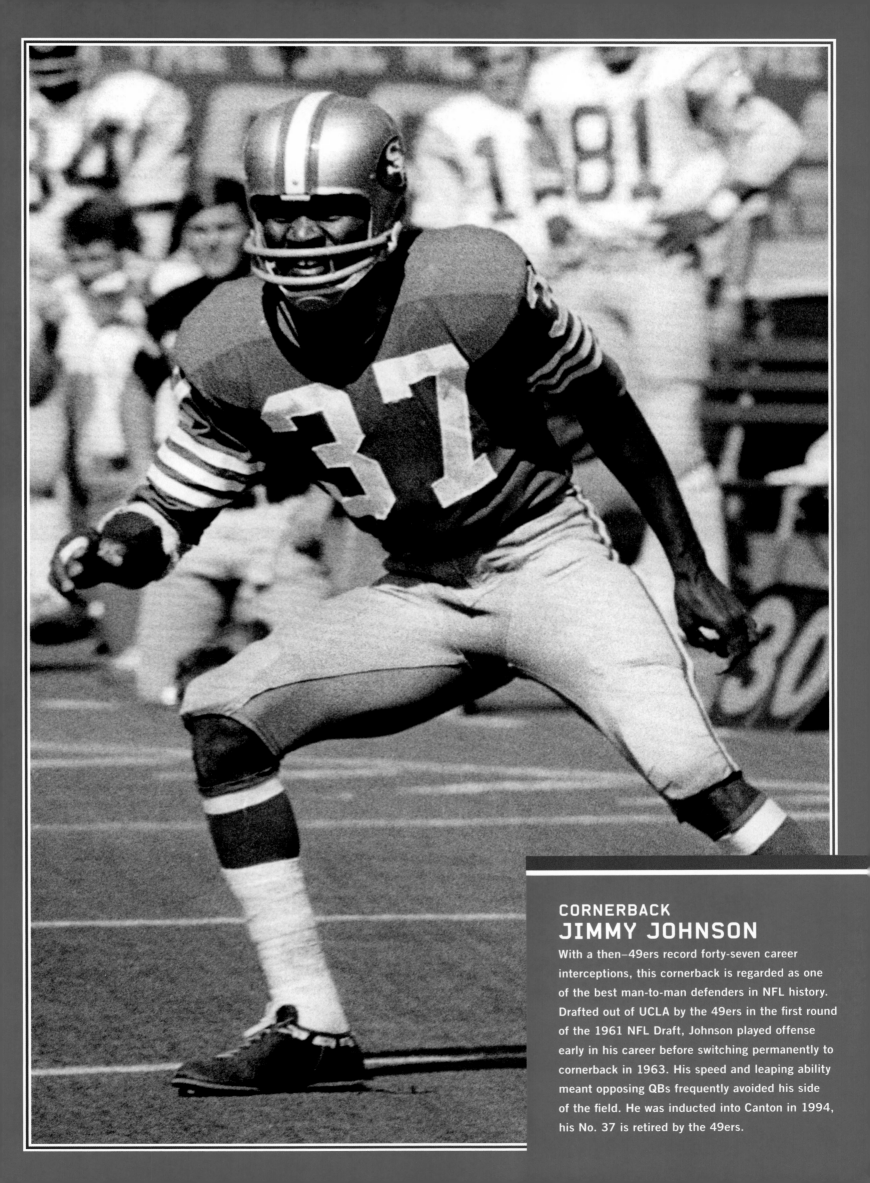

CORNERBACK
JIMMY JOHNSON

With a then–49ers record forty-seven career interceptions, this cornerback is regarded as one of the best man-to-man defenders in NFL history. Drafted out of UCLA by the 49ers in the first round of the 1961 NFL Draft, Johnson played offense early in his career before switching permanently to cornerback in 1963. His speed and leaping ability meant opposing QBs frequently avoided his side of the field. He was inducted into Canton in 1994, his No. 37 is retired by the 49ers.

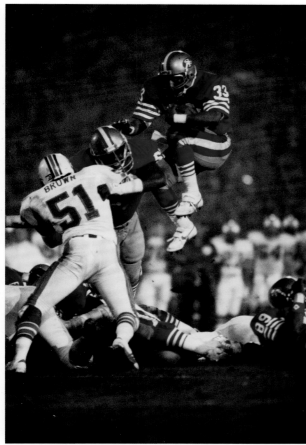

OPPOSITE: John Taylor on a punt return at Candlestick vs. Washington Redskins, September 16, 1990

ABOVE: Roger Craig leaps for a touchdown behind Guy McIntyre's block during Superbowl XIX vs. Miami Dolphins, January 20, 1985. Final score: 49ers 38, Dolphins 16

RIGHT: Eddie DeBartolo Jr., November 2, 1980

By 1979, Candlestick had served to provide a new stage for the city's beloved team, but one thing hadn't changed in the move from Kezar: the futility of losing. Something needed to change, and change it did in the biggest of ways when the man considered by many to be the most important in 49ers history arrived on the scene.

That year, Stanford's Bill Walsh was hired as the eleventh head coach in franchise history, and perhaps coincidentally, natural grass was also installed back on Candlestick's field for the same season. The moves were jointly symbolic: Life had returned to Candlestick's turf in more ways than one.

Walsh was hired by the team's brash new owner, a man named Eddie DeBartolo Jr., the son of a self-made Youngstown, Ohio, construction titan and shopping center magnate. DeBartolo bought the team from the Morabito family in 1977, becoming the team's second owner in franchise history. DeBartolo brought with him the baggage of an outsider to a famously provincial town. Skepticism ran rampant about DeBartolo's organization, especially when the team went 5–9 in 1977, and then, after the NFL debuted the league's new sixteen-game schedule, the 49ers went 2–14 in 1978.

DeBartolo's general manager, Joe Thomas, made blunder after blunder, and Candlestick's hardy fans were keen to it, hanging a bedsheet banner at Candlestick that read: "Blame Joe Thomas," which Thomas ordered taken down.

Then DeBartolo ousted Thomas and hired Bill Walsh in 1979, and it was as if the championship-free clouds that had hovered over the 49ers since 1946 parted, and heavenly rays of glorious football shone down on Candlestick Park. The 49ers launched a dynasty in the 1980s and 1990s that would include five Super Bowl championships, sixteen consecutive 10-win seasons, thirteen division titles, and the most regular-season wins of any NFL team in those decades. By any measure, the 49ers transformed into one of America's most famous and successful pro sports franchises, and coach Bill Walsh and quarterback Joe Montana were the two primary reasons why.

Walsh's touch was golden. He transformed the team with his installation of the famous "West Coast Offense," featuring quick passes and precise execution, and he had an uncanny eye for drafting talent —like Joe Montana, Ronnie Lott, and Jerry Rice—and for assembling a brilliant coaching staff, such as offensive line coach Bobb McKittrick and the defensive experts George Seifert and Bill McPherson. Walsh demanded the best, created an atmosphere of both fear and camaraderie, and outfoxed nearly every coach he faced.

"He found people with the highest ability in any field and chose them to be on his team," said tight end Russ Francis. "When you were selected by Bill Walsh, you knew that you had reached a point in your life where you got just this short moment in time to execute at that highest level.

"Bill was a genius. Bill was a great coach. But most importantly to us, he was a great human being. He was a man of all seasons."

Said Seifert, who succeeded Walsh as head coach in 1989 and would win two Super Bowls: "Bill was very complex. He was very, very competitive. He loved football and understood the game probably as well as any man I've ever met. The years I worked for Bill as an assistant were probably the happiest time of my coaching career, actually."

The 49ers launched a dynasty in the 1980s and 1990s that would include five Super Bowl championships, sixteen consecutive 10-win seasons, thirteen division titles, and the most regular-season wins of any NFL team in those decades.

BELOW: Defensive coordinator George Seifert with defense at halftime vs. Houston Oilers, October 21, 1984

PAGES 124–125: Keena Turner addresses team before taking to the field against the Los Angeles Rams on October 28, 1984. The 49ers bested the Rams 33-0.

OWNER
EDDIE DeBARTOLO JR.

The man who owned the team when it won five Super Bowls, and the first owner to do so, DeBartolo is considered one of the most successful owners in NFL history, if not all of American sports. Known equally for his passionate desire to win and his family-style embrace of players on a personal level, DeBartolo is the man who hired Bill Walsh and changed the franchise's history. Under DeBartolo, the 49ers won thirteen division titles and twenty-two playoff games.

TOP: From left to right: Roger Craig, John Ayers, Keith Fahnhorst, Fred Quillan, and Bubba Paris vs. Tampa Bay, November 18, 1984

ABOVE: Joe Montana and Bill Walsh vs. Dallas Cowboys, December 19, 1983

PAGES 128–129: In the huddle during Super Bowl XXIV vs. Denver Broncos

In the 1979 NFL draft, Walsh used the eighty-second overall pick to select Notre Dame quarterback Joe Montana. Perhaps the greatest coach-QB combination in NFL history was born.

The 49ers dynasty officially began on January 10, 1982, a date that in 49ers circles is commonly considered the way July 4, 1776, is considered in American history circles, and July 20, 1969, is considered in moon-landing circles. But Montana and Walsh actually offered a preview two years prior to that pivotal 1982 game that indicated something special was brewing.

In a meaningless game on December 7, 1980, the 49ers trailed NFC West rival New Orleans, 35–7, at halftime. At that point the 49ers had a record of 5–8, making the season another stinker in a decade full of them. And yet, inside the locker room, Walsh urged the team to continue its game plan, to attack the Saints. The team listened. In front of many empty seats and an announced attendance of 37,949, the 49ers put together what was at the time the greatest comeback in NFL history: They scored 31 unanswered points and won the game, 38–35. The Faithful who stayed at Candlestick Park on that 48-degree day, rather than leave to go Christmas shopping, roared their approval. The stadium shook with life. The quarterback, wearing No. 16, was clearly something special. One of his early offensive lineman, Dan Audick, took note.

"He'd step into the huddle, look to the receivers, make a comment, call the play, step to the line of scrimmage," Audick said. "His nickname is Joe Cool. . . . He's a pretty cool guy."

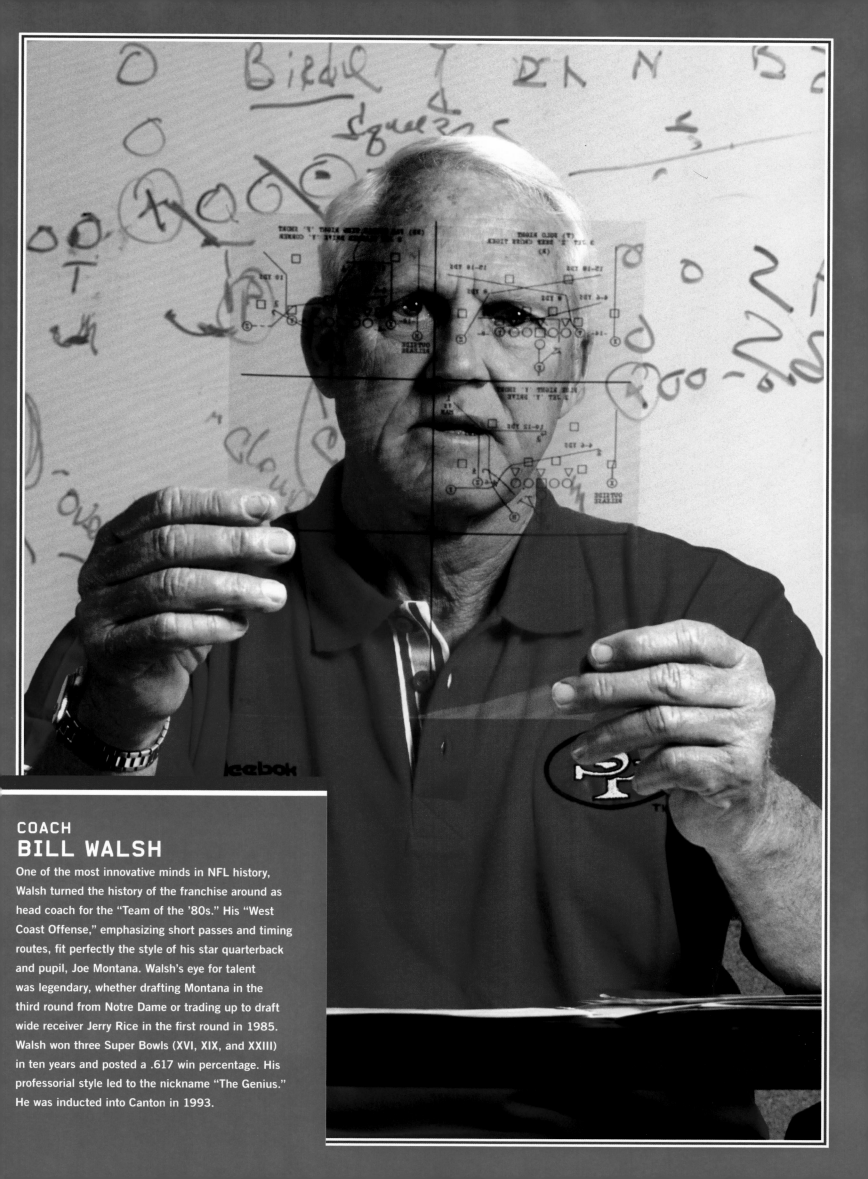

COACH
BILL WALSH

One of the most innovative minds in NFL history, Walsh turned the history of the franchise around as head coach for the "Team of the '80s." His "West Coast Offense," emphasizing short passes and timing routes, fit perfectly the style of his star quarterback and pupil, Joe Montana. Walsh's eye for talent was legendary, whether drafting Montana in the third round from Notre Dame or trading up to draft wide receiver Jerry Rice in the first round in 1985. Walsh won three Super Bowls (XVI, XIX, and XXIII) in ten years and posted a .617 win percentage. His professorial style led to the nickname "The Genius." He was inducted into Canton in 1993.

QUARTERBACK
JOE MONTANA

Quite simply the most iconic player in team history, the signal caller drafted out of Notre Dame in the third round of the 1979 NFL Draft became the man who quarterbacked the 49ers to four Super Bowl victories, winning MVP honors in Super Bowls XVI, XIX, and XXIV. The one Super Bowl he didn't win MVP, Super Bowl XXIII (Jerry Rice won it), Montana led the team on a 92-yard game-winning drive in the final moments, finding John Taylor for the winning touchdown. Perhaps Montana's most famous moment wasn't even in a Super Bowl. He threw "The Catch" to Dwight Clark to win the 1981 NFC Championship and launch the 49ers dynasty. A perfect fit for coach Bill Walsh's "West Coast Offense", Montana led thirty-one fourth-quarter comebacks and won the Associated Press NFL MVP awards in 1989 and 1990. He retired as the highest-rated QB in NFL history. He was inducted into Canton in 2000; his No. 16 jersey is retired by the 49ers.

Said Harry Sydney, a teammate in the 1980s: "It's just how they're born, man. You can't teach that, can't coach that. Either you have it, or you don't. And he had it.

"Did he throw an incredibly strong ball? No. Did he have an incredible arm? No. But he knew who to throw it to, and he knew how to throw it." Never was that more evident than on January 10, 1982.

Montana and the 49ers faced the Dallas Cowboys—there was that team again—in the NFC Championship at Candlestick, which on that sunny but brisk winter Sunday was a cauldron of organic energy, bedsheet signs, and early 1980s fashion: trucker hats, satin jackets, cigarettes, and no cell phones. At halftime, entertainment was provided by the local rock/pop band the Tubes. They played on a flatbed truck in the north end zone. Then came history.

Only fifty-eight seconds remained in the game. The 49ers were trailing, 27–21, and facing third-and-3 from the Dallas 6-yard line, after having driven across the painted 49ers helmet at midfield and down the splotchy turf, which was soaked by January rains. Walsh called timeout and told Montana, as placidly as if it were a July training camp day in Rocklin, California, "We're going to run a 'Sprint Right Option.'" That meant Montana would roll right and look for Freddie Solomon as his primary receiver underneath the defensive coverage. If Solomon wasn't open, Dwight Clark was to slide across the back of the north end zone. Somehow, Montana, under great duress, and after a pump fake—his eyes fixed on the end zone, his youthful blonde hair jutting out the back of his helmet—threw the ball off his back foot to where only Clark could catch it.

"Did he throw an incredibly strong ball? No. Did he have an incredible arm? No. But he knew who to throw it to, and he knew how to throw it."

ABOVE: Joe Montana addressing team after their 1989 NFC Divisional Playoff win vs. Minnesota Vikings

PAGES 132–133: The Catch, January 10, 1982

Clark jumped and made "The Catch."

"The only spot it could be," said Clark. "[Dallas defensive back] Everson Walls would have jumped up and battled me for the ball, but instead he thought it was going out of bounds. That allowed me to jump up and catch it uncontested."

Part of Montana's appeal to his teammates was his lack of on-field ego. Asked about "The Catch," Montana instead focused on to two other things: the 49ers defense and his own mistakes. "Everyone thinks of that game as 'The Catch,' but in reality it should have been called 'The Tackle,' with Eric Wright's stop on Drew Pearson," Montana said, referring to a play on the Cowboys' ensuing drive. "If he doesn't make that tackle, they score a touchdown and we lose the game.

"I always tell people, you can't stop playing, you can't quit if you make a mistake. The play before 'The Catch,' I overthrew Freddie Solomon by three feet. He was wide open. 'The Catch' should have never happened, but I missed him. I made a mistake. But you come back and you've just got to keep playing."

By the time Clark came back to earth and spiked the football in the soggy end zone painted red with the team name "49ers" in that recognizable saloon font, Candlestick had come unhinged. CBS video from that day shows fans losing their minds, bear-hugging in the stands, a city and a team becoming one. Thirty-five years after the Morabito family created the team, and eleven years into their Candlestick tenure, the 49ers had an NFC Championship, and "The Catch" would live on as one of the team's—and certainly Candlestick Park's—greatest moments.

Compared to the modernity of Levi's Stadium today, everything about the game and moment seems so primitive. Handmade bedsheet signs hung all over Candlestick, including one near the end zone where Clark caught the ball that read "Send the Cowboys to Montana." The scoreboard, a simple black face with yellow light bulbs, flashed things like, "60,525 . . . Largest Crowd in 49ers History!!!" This was a far cry from the twenty-first-century video screens that now entertain fans in Santa Clara, and yet, the Candlestick generation would never trade the memories.

"The Catch will always be first and foremost," said Keena Turner, winner of four Super Bowl rings. "Because without it, it doesn't seem like there was a beginning."

Fans celebrate The Catch (TOP) while the Dallas Cowboys hang their heads in defeat and disbelief (ABOVE)

WIDE RECEIVER
DWIGHT CLARK

Two words – "The Catch" – define the legacy of this tenth-round draft pick from Clemson, another example of a shrewd Bill Walsh draft pick. When Clark skied over Dallas defensive back Everson Walls to pluck Joe Montana's pass from the Candlestick sky to win the 1981 NFC Championship, everything changed—in 49ers and NFL history. The wide receiver won two Super Bowls with the 49ers, made two Pro Bowls, and was first-team All-Pro twice. His jersey No. 87 is retired by the team.

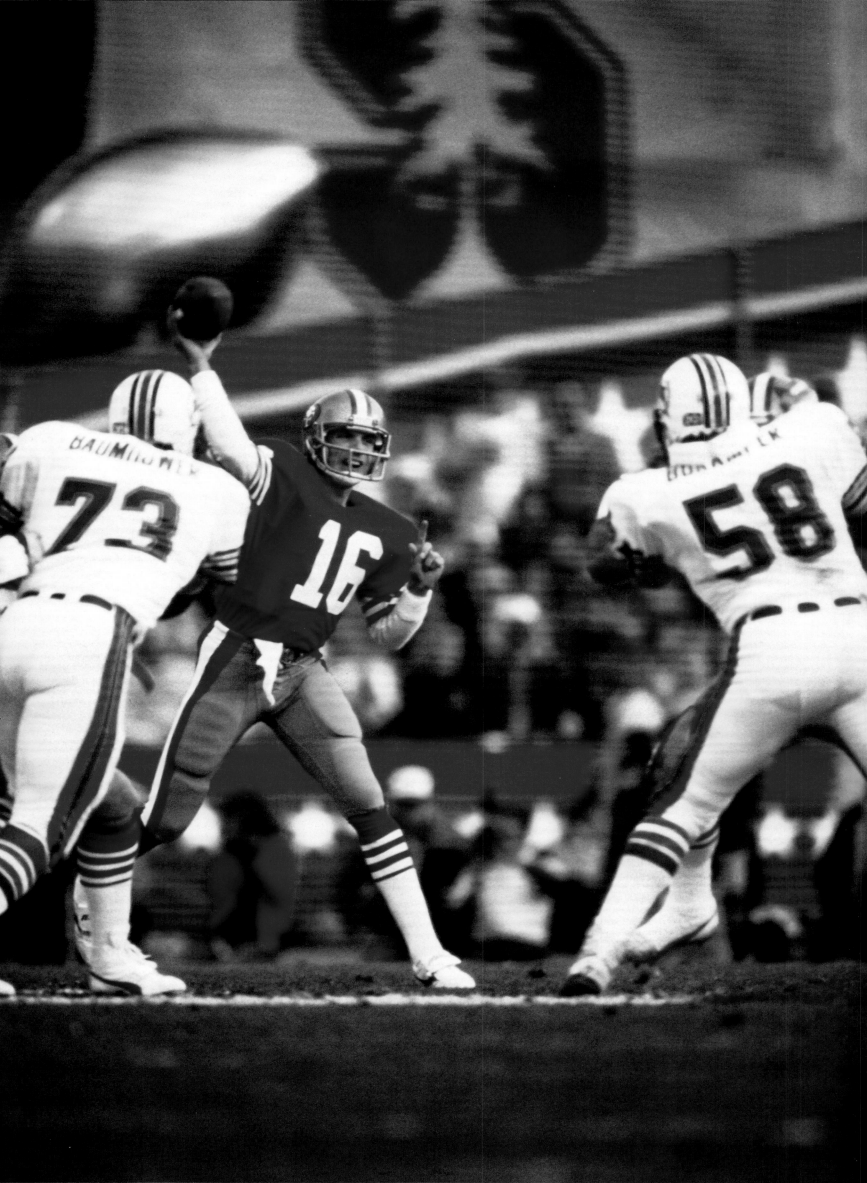

Indeed, the 49ers went on to win their first Super Bowl in 1982, a 26–21 victory over the Cincinnati Bengals, and from there, Candlestick steadily took its place as one of American sports' most important temples.

OPPOSITE: Joe Montana passes during Super Bowl XIX vs. Miami Dolphins, January 20, 1985

BELOW: Super Bowl XVI. Final score: 49ers 26, Bengals 21

Indeed, the 49ers went on to win their first Super Bowl in 1982, a 26–21 victory over the Cincinnati Bengals, and from there, Candlestick steadily took its place as one of American sports' most important temples. That it was the home of Montana and Walsh was enough, but it also held future Hall-of-Famer Ronnie Lott at safety and, in 1985, the player many consider the greatest in NFL history—wide receiver Jerry Rice. Through the 1980s, the 49ers and Candlestick became as familiar a sight on national TV as any team and stadium in the league. On CBS—and later FOX—the voices of broadcasters Pat Summerall and John Madden provided the commentary, while aerial shots of San Francisco's sights—the Golden Gate Bridge, Alcatraz, cable cars—provided the backdrop to the 49ers dominance. Aerials of Candlestick would show that familiar concrete oblong in the southeastern end of the city filled to the brim—once the team started winning, they rarely drew fewer than 60,000 to the 'Stick. National anthems sung by 49ers fanatics Huey Lewis and the News, and R&B artist Jeffrey Osborne, became staples.

In January 1985, the 49ers won the NFC Championship at Candlestick, shutting out the Chicago Bears, 23–0, en route to a second Super Bowl title. This they won just down the road at Stanford in a game that fueled Montana's growing legend, as he outdueled the great Dan Marino in an MVP-winning 38–16 blowout. In January 1989, the 49ers won their third Super Bowl, 20–16, in a rematch with the Cincinnati Bengals. And in January 1990, the 49ers won the NFC Championship at Candlestick, crushing the rival Los Angeles Rams, 30–3, en route to a fourth Super Bowl title, a 55–10 obliteration of Denver down in New Orleans.

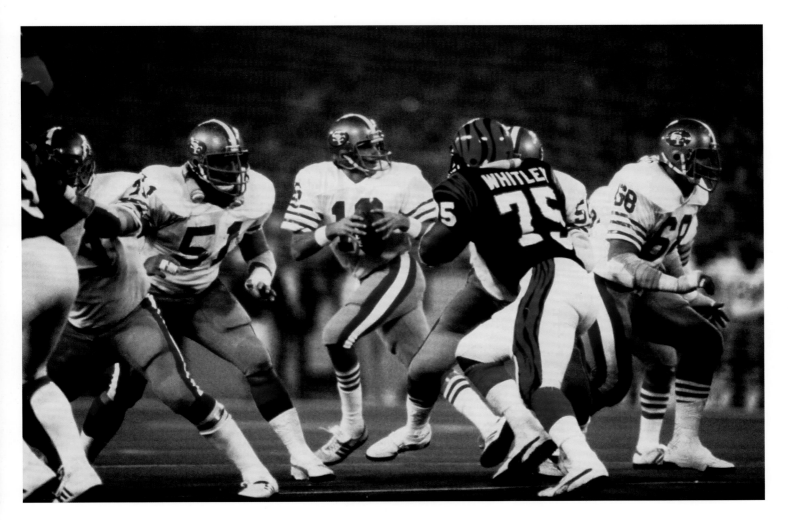

TOP: Super Bowl XXIII parade in San Francisco, California, January 22, 1989

ABOVE: Steve Young scrambles during 1995 NFC Divisional Playoffs vs. Chicago Bears. 49ers took the win 44 to 15.

Joe Montana was not the only 49ers quarterback to find glory amid Candlestick's damp, concrete charm. In 1987, the team made a trade with the Tampa Bay Buccaneers that brought quarterback Steve Young to the 49ers—a move orchestrated by Bill Walsh to exert maximum pressure on Joe Montana later in his career. Not surprisingly, this situation led to much attendant drama—and Young's initial years with the 49ers were alternately exhilarating and maddening. Maddening when he and Montana descended into a locker room Cold War; as Young said, "I don't think it's possible to capture the drama that went on, and it was authored by Bill." And exhilarating when Young did things like zig, zag, and scramble for 49 yards on a legendary TD run against the Minnesota Vikings on October 30, 1988. This game at Candlestick, a 24–21 win, became key in a season that ended with another Montana-led Super Bowl.

Called by the legendarily deep pipes of 49ers radio man Lon Simmons, Young's epic run sounded like this: "Young, back to throw. . . . In trouble, he's going to be sacked! . . . No, gets away! . . . He runs, gets away again! . . . Goes to the 40, gets away again! . . . To the 35, cuts back at the 30! . . . To the 20, the 15, the 10, he *dives* . . . touchdown, 49ers!"

Young said, by the end of his scramble, "My body realized that I was cooked. I had nothing left, and almost collapsed as I fell. My legs just quit. If it had been 10 more yards, my nose would have ended up in the dirt. It's kind of kooky, but it's a fun piece of history."

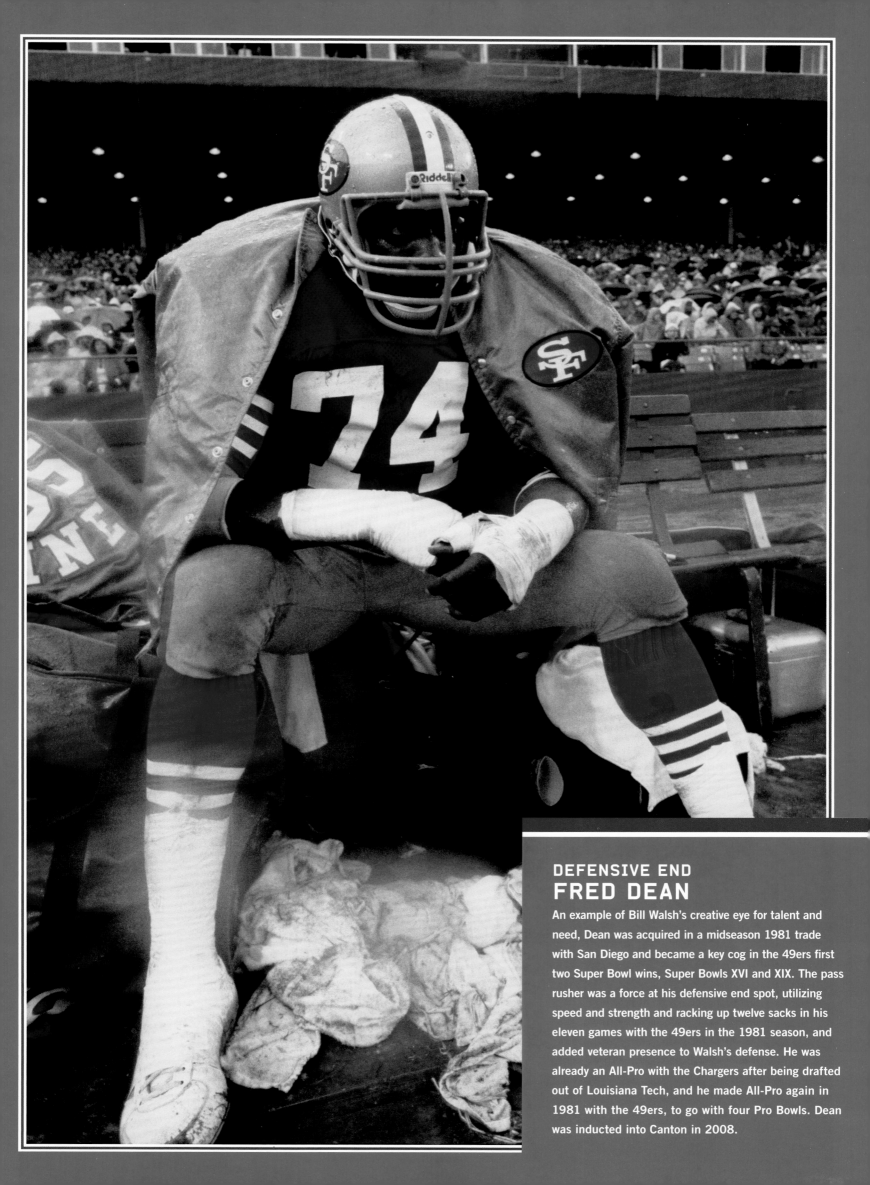

DEFENSIVE END
FRED DEAN

An example of Bill Walsh's creative eye for talent and need, Dean was acquired in a midseason 1981 trade with San Diego and became a key cog in the 49ers first two Super Bowl wins, Super Bowls XVI and XIX. The pass rusher was a force at his defensive end spot, utilizing speed and strength and racking up twelve sacks in his eleven games with the 49ers in the 1981 season, and added veteran presence to Walsh's defense. He was already an All-Pro with the Chargers after being drafted out of Louisiana Tech, and he made All-Pro again in 1981 with the 49ers, to go with four Pro Bowls. Dean was inducted into Canton in 2008.

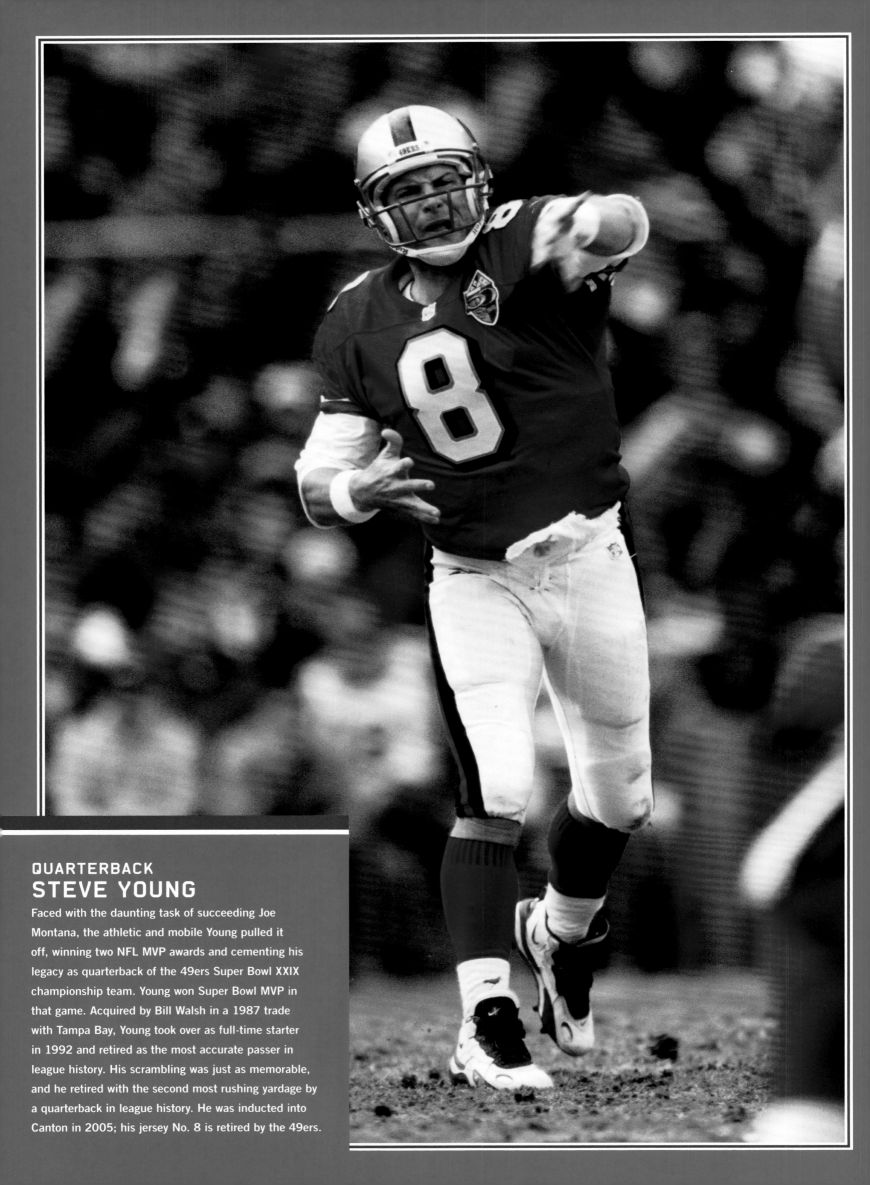

QUARTERBACK
STEVE YOUNG

Faced with the daunting task of succeeding Joe Montana, the athletic and mobile Young pulled it off, winning two NFL MVP awards and cementing his legacy as quarterback of the 49ers Super Bowl XXIX championship team. Young won Super Bowl MVP in that game. Acquired by Bill Walsh in a 1987 trade with Tampa Bay, Young took over as full-time starter in 1992 and retired as the most accurate passer in league history. His scrambling was just as memorable, and he retired with the second most rushing yardage by a quarterback in league history. He was inducted into Canton in 2005; his jersey No. 8 is retired by the 49ers.

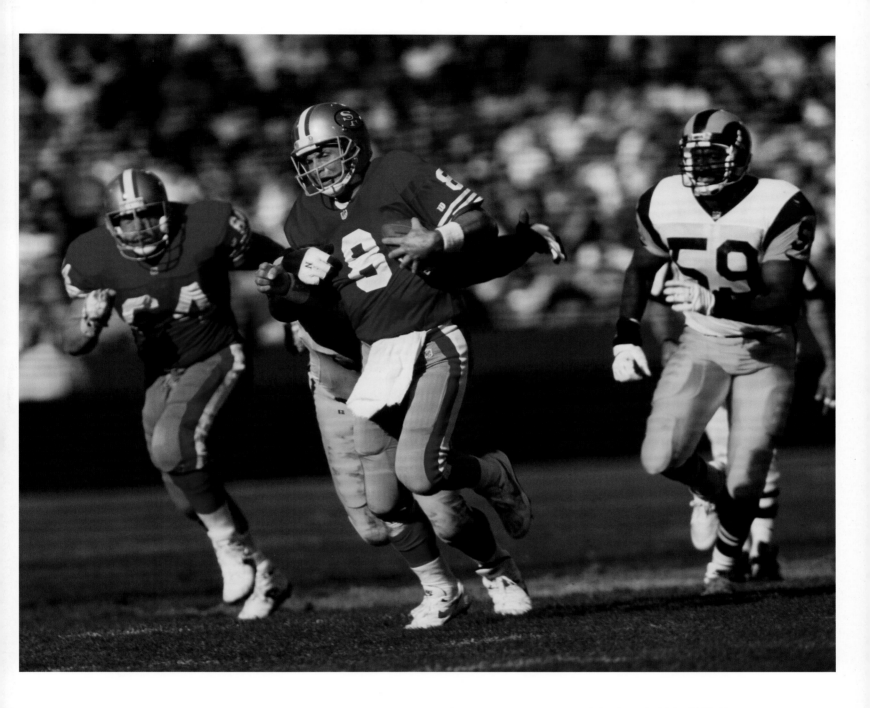

During the 1991 season, Montana had elbow surgery, which opened the door for Young to take over at quarterback. Then at the end of the 1992 season, in January 1993, the 49ers again met the Cowboys in the NFC Championship game at Candlestick, with Young at the helm. However, even as the 49ers were losing, Montana stood on the sidelines, in uniform and able to play, but then-coach George Seifert never used him in the game. The writing was on the wall. In the ensuing offseason, the 49ers traded Joe Montana to Kansas City.

The 1993 season ended the same way: with a loss to the Cowboys in the January 1994 NFC Championship game. Then, in 1994, it happened again: For the third season in a row, the 49ers and Young found themselves facing the rival Cowboys to determine the NFC Champion, and it was clear that the teams were locked in a titanic struggle for dominance, as the red-and-gold combatants vied with the blue-and-white from the Lone Star State for the same prize. The date was January 15, 1995, but it might as well have been renamed the Most Important Date in Steve Young's Life. After six seasons leading the 49ers, he had yet to lead them to a championship.

ᴛᴏᴘ: Steve Young scrambles against the
Los Angeles Rams.

> It was clear that the teams were locked in a titanic struggle for dominance, as the red-and-gold combatants vied with the blue-and-white from the Lone Star State for the same prize.

As Seifert would later say, Candlestick became "unglued" as Young finally vanquished Troy Aikman and the Cowboys, winning the 1995 championship, 38–28. Young's postgame exultation was one of Candlestick's most memorable moments, a man finally shedding the burden of Montana's considerable legacy, as a Candlestick crowd chanted "Steve! Steve! Steve!"—a chant of love and apology all wrapped up in one. A security guard tried to corral Young to keep him from running into the masses that swarmed the field, but like his 1988 run against the Vikings, Young's legs and heart would not be denied.

"I had never felt better," Young said of that late-afternoon, postgame celebration. "I mean, when I was running around Candlestick Park, I ended up doing all these kind of strange things that were just . . . I didn't even think about it. I started running around the stadium. I just lost my mind a little bit because of the import of what just happened."

The whole 1994 season was one of the 49ers most epic in its Candlestick years. It ended with Young mania and another Super Bowl win—making the 49ers the first team to win five Super Bowls—but the magical ride began about four months earlier on September 5, 1994. In the Monday Night Football season opener, the 49ers faced the Los Angeles Raiders, and Jerry Rice, maybe the greatest player of all time, caught three TDs to become the NFL's all-time leading touchdown scorer.

TOP: George Seifert

LEFT: Jesse Sapolu, NFC Championship vs. Dallas Cowboys, January 15, 1995

ABOVE: Ricky Watters, NFC Championship vs. Dallas Cowboys, January 15, 1995

OPPOSITE: Jerry Rice and Steve Young vs. Detroit Lions, December 19, 1993

PAGES 144–145: Steve Young scrambles for a touchdown during the 1995 NFC Divisional Playoff game against the Chicago Bears. 49ers win 44 to 15.

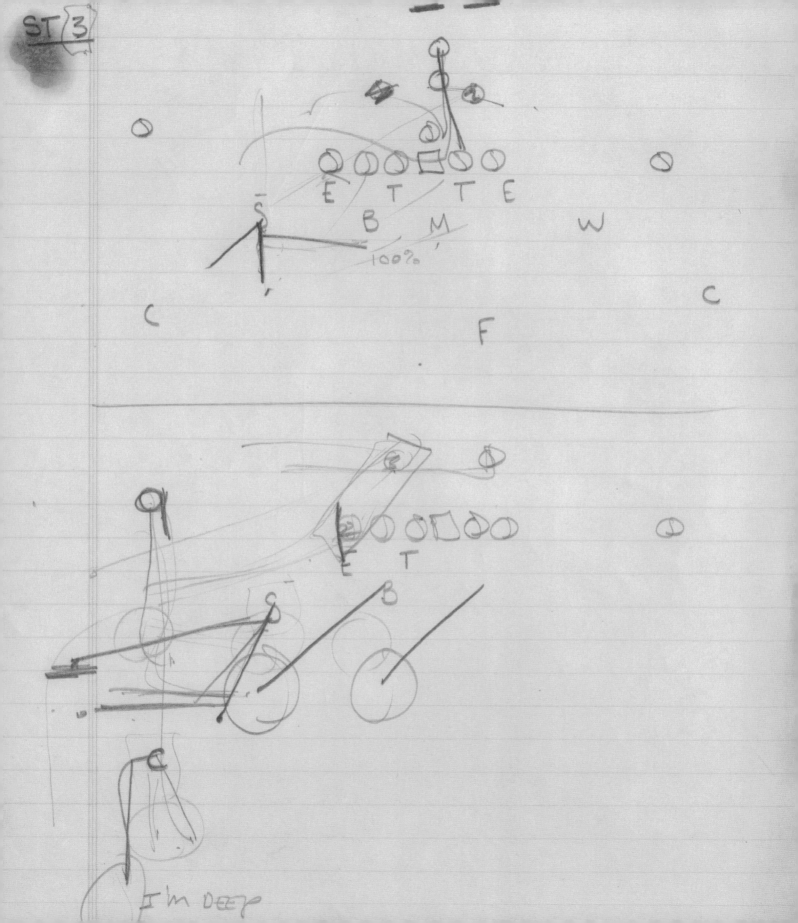

E   T   T   E

S

B   M   W

100%

C

F

C

E

T

B

C

I'M DEEP

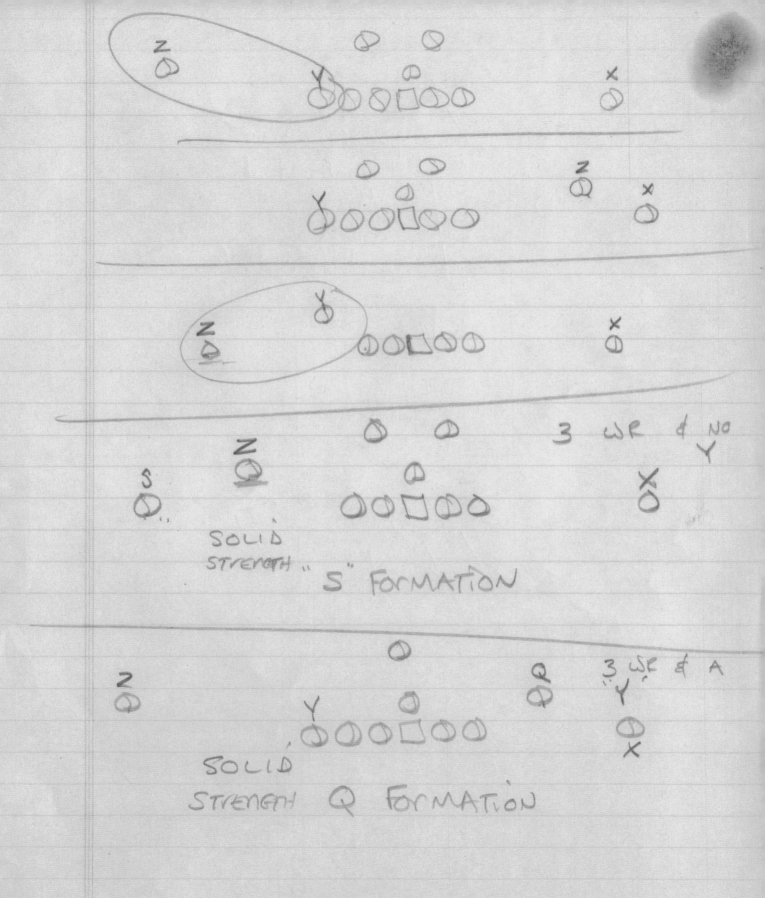

"S" FORMATION

SOLID STRENGTH

SOLID STRENGTH Q FORMATION

TOP: Jerry Rice addresses the team before Super Bowl XXIX vs. San Diego Chargers

ABOVE: Jerry Rice makes his 127th touchdown reception against the Oakland Raiders on September 5, 1994, breaking the NFL record.

Jerry Rice's run with the 49ers from 1985 to 2000 was nothing short of the greatest in league history. He set records in Beamonesque fashion, so distant from their peers as if never to be broken. His 208 career TDs are the best of all time, and the 187 TDs he scored with the 49ers alone would stand on their own as the greatest number of TDs by one player in history, ahead of Emmitt Smith's 175.

Rice's greatness consistently dazzled even his NFL teammates, who marveled at his obsession with perfection, his relentless work ethic, and his unquenchable desire to be the best. By the time Rice arrived, Montana had two Super Bowl championships, but Joe still marveled at the wide receiver. "All he did was get behind defenders," said Montana, who threw Rice 11 passes for 215 yards in the 1989 Super Bowl, which earned Rice the game's MVP award. "I don't care who it was. He'd get behind safeties."

After Montana left, Steve Young combined with Rice to form the most prolific quarterback/receiver touchdown duo in NFL history. "He acted like a guy who just barely made it into the league," Young said, "and that never stopped."

He didn't stop on that September night in the 1994 opener. First, he burned the Raiders for a 69-yard TD from Young for No. 125, and then a 23-yard rush made it No. 126, tying Jim Brown atop the all-time NFL touchdown list. And he wasn't done. The nation was watching, and the 49ers were up 37–14 in the fourth quarter, when Seifert approached Rice on the sidelines. "I'm going to give you guys one more opportunity to do it, here at home, in Candlestick Park," Seifert said.

Rice, who thought he'd been removed from the game to rest because of the blowout, grabbed his helmet and ran back out onto the Candlestick turf, under those Candlestick lights, to the delight of the sellout crowd.

From the 38-yard line, Young took the snap and dropped back. Rice streaked toward the end zone. The ball lofted from Young's left arm and sailed through the San Francisco night.

"Everything that Bill Walsh had taught me—catch the ball at its highest peak, go and attack the football—I remembered," Rice said, and he soared, and "everything slowed down just a little bit, and I was able to go up and make that catch and come down with that football, and that was No. 127 and that broke Jim Brown's record." Candlestick roared. Another moment in the old bowl's history, emblazoned in memory.

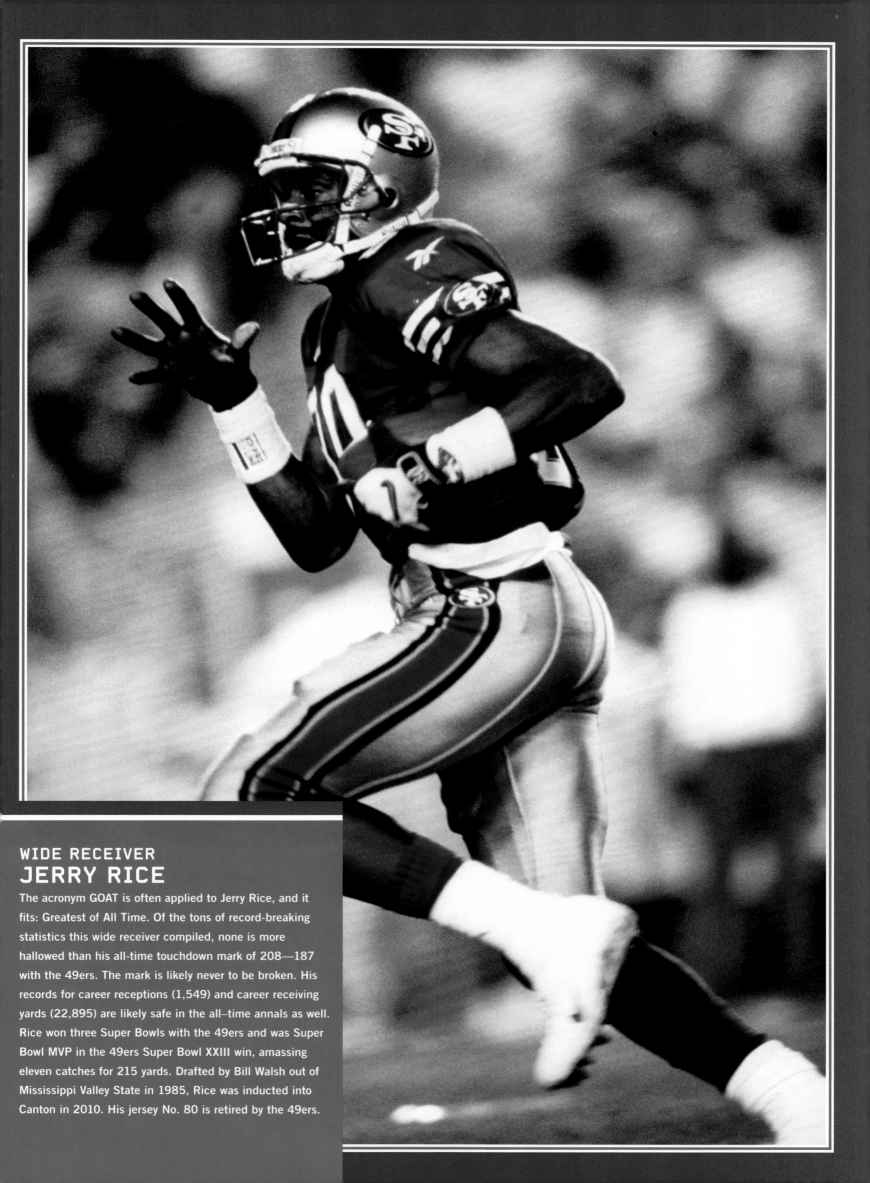

WIDE RECEIVER
JERRY RICE

The acronym GOAT is often applied to Jerry Rice, and it fits: Greatest of All Time. Of the tons of record-breaking statistics this wide receiver compiled, none is more hallowed than his all-time touchdown mark of 208—187 with the 49ers. The mark is likely never to be broken. His records for career receptions (1,549) and career receiving yards (22,895) are likely safe in the all-time annals as well. Rice won three Super Bowls with the 49ers and was Super Bowl MVP in the 49ers Super Bowl XXIII win, amassing eleven catches for 215 yards. Drafted by Bill Walsh out of Mississippi Valley State in 1985, Rice was inducted into Canton in 2010. His jersey No. 80 is retired by the 49ers.

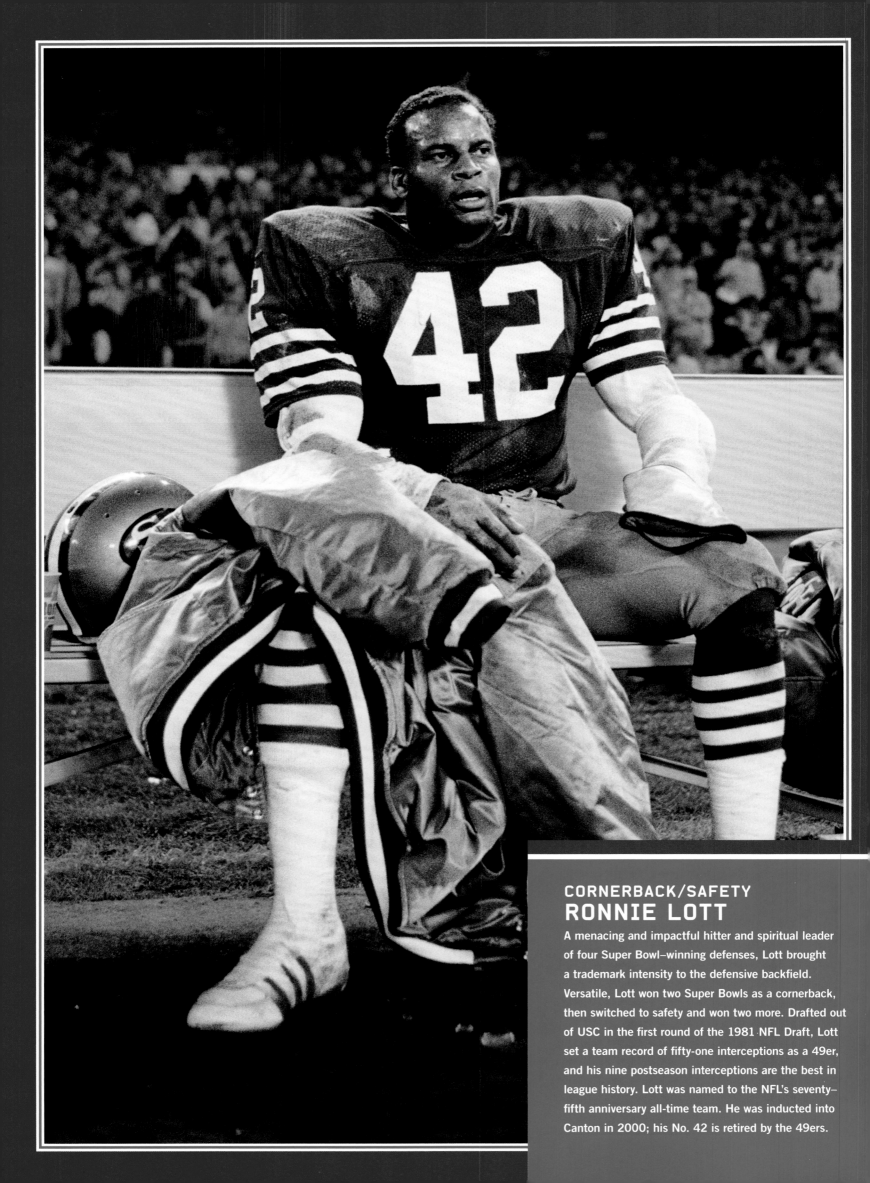

CORNERBACK/SAFETY
RONNIE LOTT

A menacing and impactful hitter and spiritual leader of four Super Bowl–winning defenses, Lott brought a trademark intensity to the defensive backfield. Versatile, Lott won two Super Bowls as a cornerback, then switched to safety and won two more. Drafted out of USC in the first round of the 1981 NFL Draft, Lott set a team record of fifty-one interceptions as a 49er, and his nine postseason interceptions are the best in league history. Lott was named to the NFL's seventy-fifth anniversary all-time team. He was inducted into Canton in 2000; his No. 42 is retired by the 49ers.

Four years after that, another receiver made another catch that was so dramatic it has commonly been called "The Catch 2." In the late 1990s, the 49ers struggled with a new nemesis, the Green Bay Packers. Brett Favre's crew, coached by former 49ers offensive coordinator Mike Holmgren, another Bill Walsh coaching protégé, knocked the 49ers out of the playoffs in 1995, 1996, and most painfully, in the 1997 NFC Championship game at Candlestick Park. This 1997 game ruined the otherwise promising first year of the 49ers gregarious new head coach, Steve Mariucci.

In 1998, the 49ers couldn't bear the thought of losing to the Packers and their Cheesehead fans a fourth consecutive year. They faced them in an NFC wild-card playoff game on January 3, 1999, and were trailing, 27–23, with eight seconds left. On Green Bay's 25-yard line, Steve Young took the snap, stumbled once, regained his footing, and fired a pass that offensive line coach Bobb McKittrick later called "the greatest pass I've ever seen." The ball split the gap between Green Bay's safeties, and Terrell Owens, a mercurial talent in a No. 81 jersey, grabbed Young's seed of a pass in the end zone for a touchdown so stunning, and a vanquishing of Green Bay so redemptive, the play lives as one of Candlestick's loudest and proudest memories. "Terrell was forever thankful," Young said. "I still see him and he thanks me for that pass."

"The Catch 2" would be one of Candlestick Park's last memorable moments for more than a decade. Young's career ended with a concussion the next season, and Rice left for the Oakland Raiders after the 2000 season.

Perhaps the next best Candlestick moment occurred in the 2002 NFC wild-card game. Quarterback Jeff Garcia—another Walsh find from Walsh's alma mater San Jose State—and the 49ers were trailing the rival New York Giants by 38–14, late in the third quarter. Then Garcia orchestrated a startling comeback win, 39–38, in a game Jed York still calls his favorite. Unfortunately, the 49ers lost at Tampa Bay the next week, and Coach Mariucci was fired.

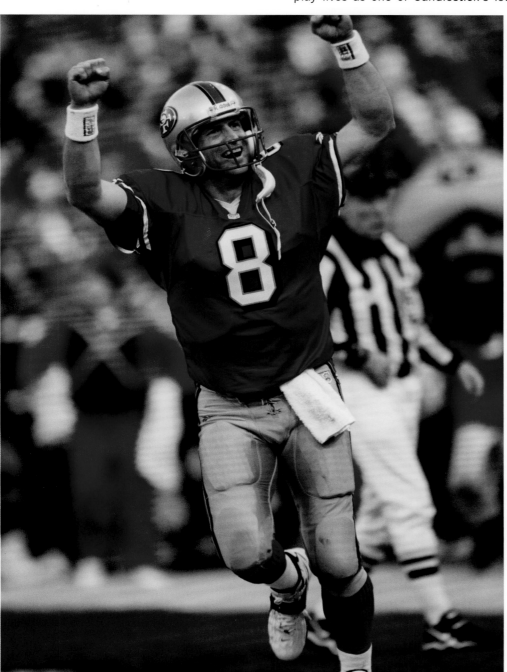

LEFT: Steve Young celebrates after completing the game-winning pass against the Green Bay Packers in the 1999 wild-card playoff game.

PAGES 150–151: Ronnie Lott picks one off against the New York Giants, January 4, 1987

The ensuing years were not good ones at Candlestick Park. The losses piled up, and 49ers football became reminiscent of the 1970s at the 'Stick or Kezar's long fruitless stretch.

Although Candlestick began to lose its life, and only the ghosts of the glory days remained, some things at Candlestick improved. The San Francisco Giants left for a new home, AT&T Park, in 1999, meaning the field at Candlestick could become football-only. No more infield dirt or patchy sod around the bases. Field drainage improved, leaving those 1980s playoff memories of soggy Candlestick behind. The 49ers could finally expand their tiny locker room into the Giants' space, making for more tolerable working quarters on fall Sundays.

But as the sports world zoomed into the twenty-first century, more and more NFL teams were building the stadium equivalents of silk purses, which made Candlestick Park look more and more like a sow's ear.

Traffic ingress and egress bothered fans. Candlestick's concourses felt cramped compared to modern stadiums. Concessions stands were woefully outdated. The 49ers watched as the Dallas Cowboys and the New England Patriots and the Seattle Seahawks and the New York Giants and the Washington Redskins built gleaming new football temples, and they itched for change.

In November 2006, they announced change was coming. The 49ers and SCSA would build a new stadium in Santa Clara, bidding farewell to over sixty years of football within San Francisco's city limits. The Santa Clara stadium would revolutionize the 49ers fan experience. But what the new stadium would really need, most of all, was a winning team.

ABOVE: Aerial of Candlestick Park

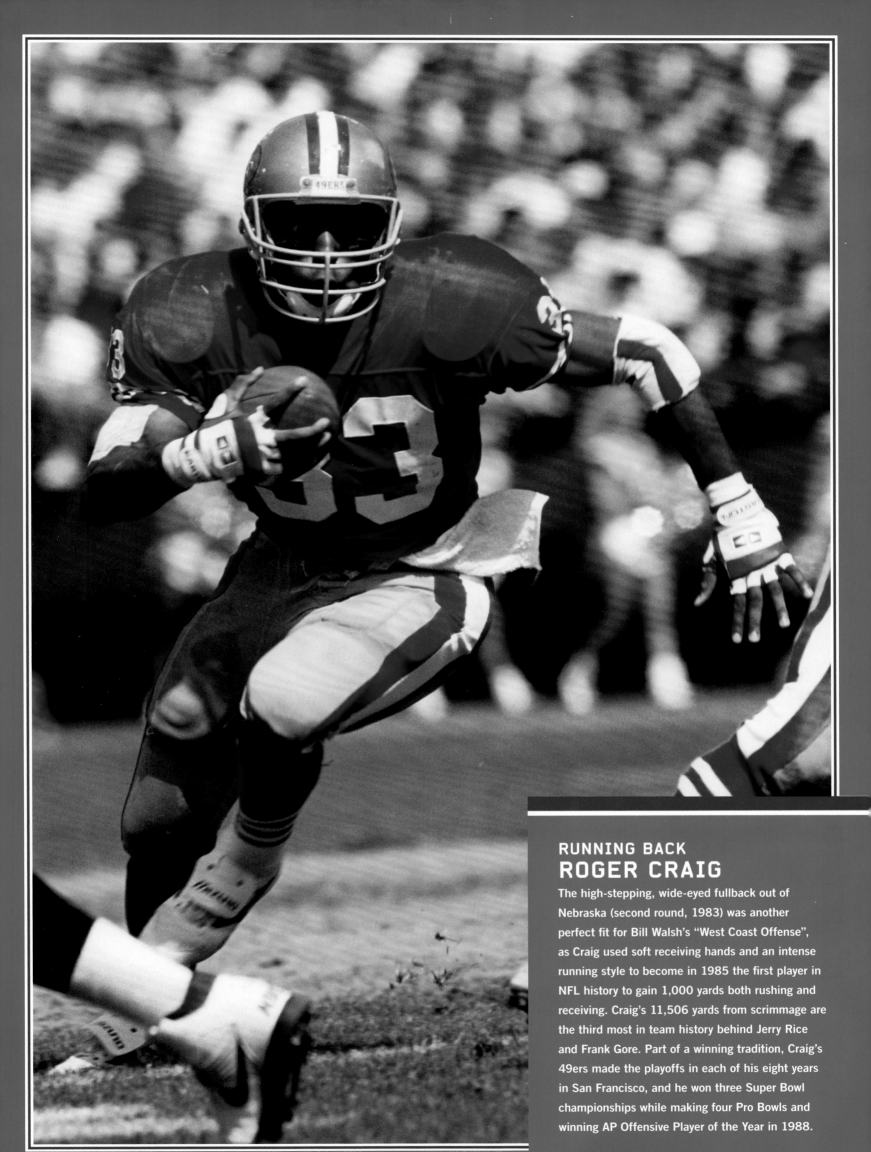

RUNNING BACK
ROGER CRAIG

The high-stepping, wide-eyed fullback out of Nebraska (second round, 1983) was another perfect fit for Bill Walsh's "West Coast Offense", as Craig used soft receiving hands and an intense running style to become in 1985 the first player in NFL history to gain 1,000 yards both rushing and receiving. Craig's 11,506 yards from scrimmage are the third most in team history behind Jerry Rice and Frank Gore. Part of a winning tradition, Craig's 49ers made the playoffs in each of his eight years in San Francisco, and he won three Super Bowl championships while making four Pro Bowls and winning AP Offensive Player of the Year in 1988.

The pass threaded coverage to reach tight end Vernon Davis, who clutched the ball as he got clobbered and scored the touchdown. Candlestick shook.

ABOVE: 49ers beat New Orleans Saints with a Vernon Davis touchdown reception in the fourth quarter of the 2012 NFC Divisional playoffs

OPPOSITE: Coach Jim Harbaugh

When Jed York, the nephew of Eddie DeBartolo Jr., hired Jim Harbaugh from Stanford as head coach in 2011, the franchise finally felt the wind in its sails again. A thoroughly different personality from the professorial Bill Walsh, Harbaugh was imbued with the adrenalized approach of a fourteen-year NFL quarterback. Yet Harbaugh's hiring was analogous to Walsh in a few important ways. He was an offensive mind. He had a track record of success. And he valued and taught the quarterback position.

While Walsh favored white sweaters, Harbaugh coached every game in a utilitarian black sweatshirt and khakis, the better, he said, to "reduce drag" in wondering what to wear every day.

Harbaugh's hiring immediately translated into wins, and this immediately produced more epic Candlestick memories, moments made more poignant because of Candlestick's imminent demise. Perhaps the most emotional was the 49ers 2012 NFC divisional win over the New Orleans Saints, a 36–32 game that not only was one of the best playoff games in recent NFL history but also served as a triumph for a player who had endured the slings and arrows of the bad 49ers years from 2005 to 2010, quarterback Alex Smith.

After being selected No. 1 out of Utah by the 49ers in 2005, Smith's career seemed doomed to failure. The 49ers never sniffed the playoffs in Smith's first six years, but Harbaugh's arrival was like a magic touch, and Smith's talents—his nimble feet and accurate arm—flourished. They never flourished more than on January 14, 2012, at Candlestick. With four minutes to play in the divisional contest, the Saints and high-powered QB Drew Brees had a 24–23 lead and things looked grim.

But Smith led a six-play, 80-yard TD drive that he capped with a startling and thrilling bootleg, a 29-yard scoring run with 2:18 left that had Candlestick's Faithful roaring like the old days. This was the first playoff glory since Jeff Garcia led the comeback against the Giants nine years earlier. In the KNBR radio booth, play-by-play man Ted Robinson exulted as Smith crossed the goal line, calling it "the play of dreams!" The 49ers led, 29–24.

Then the Saints answered with a lightning bolt, as Brees completed a 66-yard TD pass to Jimmy Graham, and the Saints led, 32–29, with 1:37 left. Could Smith channel his inner Joe Montana? The answer, incredibly, was yes. Smith led the 49ers from their own 15-yard line to the Saints' 14-yard line with fourteen seconds left. In the huddle, he called "Vernon Post" and threw a dart worthy of Young-to-Owens: The pass threaded coverage to reach tight end Vernon Davis, who clutched the ball as he got clobbered and scored the touchdown. Candlestick shook. "Don't ever," an exultant Robinson exhorted in the broadcast booth, "doubt Alex Smith again!" The 49ers won, 36–32. San Francisco's football glory was back.

The next year, Smith was replaced by Colin Kaepernick, Harbaugh's hand-picked new quarterback, a six-foot-four stallion of an athlete who brought a new-age skill set of size, speed, and strength. Kaepernick led the 49ers back to the NFC divisional playoffs where, on January 12, 2013, he charged past the Green Bay Packers—again, a Candlestick thread—for a 45–31 win. In the game, Kaepernick didn't stop running until he had set an NFL record of 181 yards rushing by a quarterback.

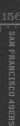

ABOVE: Alex Smith runs one in against the Saints in the fourth quarter of the 2012 NFC Divisional playoffs

OPPOSITE: Vernon Davis and Frank Gore celebrate in the final minutes of the 2012 NFC Divisional playoff win against the New Orleans Saints

But first, the 49ers had to say good-bye to Candlestick Park. They did, on December 23, 2013, the night NaVorro Bowman made the interception known as the "Pick at the 'Stick," leading to a victory laden with cheers and nostalgia.

ABOVE: Anthony Davis blocks for Colin Kaepernick as he sets up for a pass against the Seattle Seahawks, December 8, 2013

PAGES 160–161: NaVorro Bowman's "Pick at the 'Stick" during the final game at Candlestick Park against the Atlanta Falcons

Then 'Kap' did Alex Smith one better. He led the 49ers to victory in the championship game and into the 2013 Super Bowl, where the 49ers fell just short of the Baltimore Ravens, losing 34–31. Kap seemed to be streaking into the 49ers future and was a lock to lead the team into Levi's Stadium for the 2014 season.

But first, the 49ers had to say good-bye to Candlestick Park. They did, on December 23, 2013, the night NaVorro Bowman made the interception known as the "Pick at the 'Stick," leading to a victory laden with cheers and nostalgia. After the game, on the field, Boyz II Men, a longtime DeBartolo family favorite, sang "It's So Hard to Say Goodbye to Yesterday." Fireworks lit up the sky.

Longtime Candlestick employees gathered on the field and took pictures. Fans chanted throughout the game, a rhythmic tribute, "Can-dle-stick! Can-dle-stick!" Keena Turner arrived early that day and took a personal tour, heading to nooks and crannies and offices he never saw as a player. Candlestick Park—maligned, outdated, and filled with a city's heartwarming memories—was on display one last time.

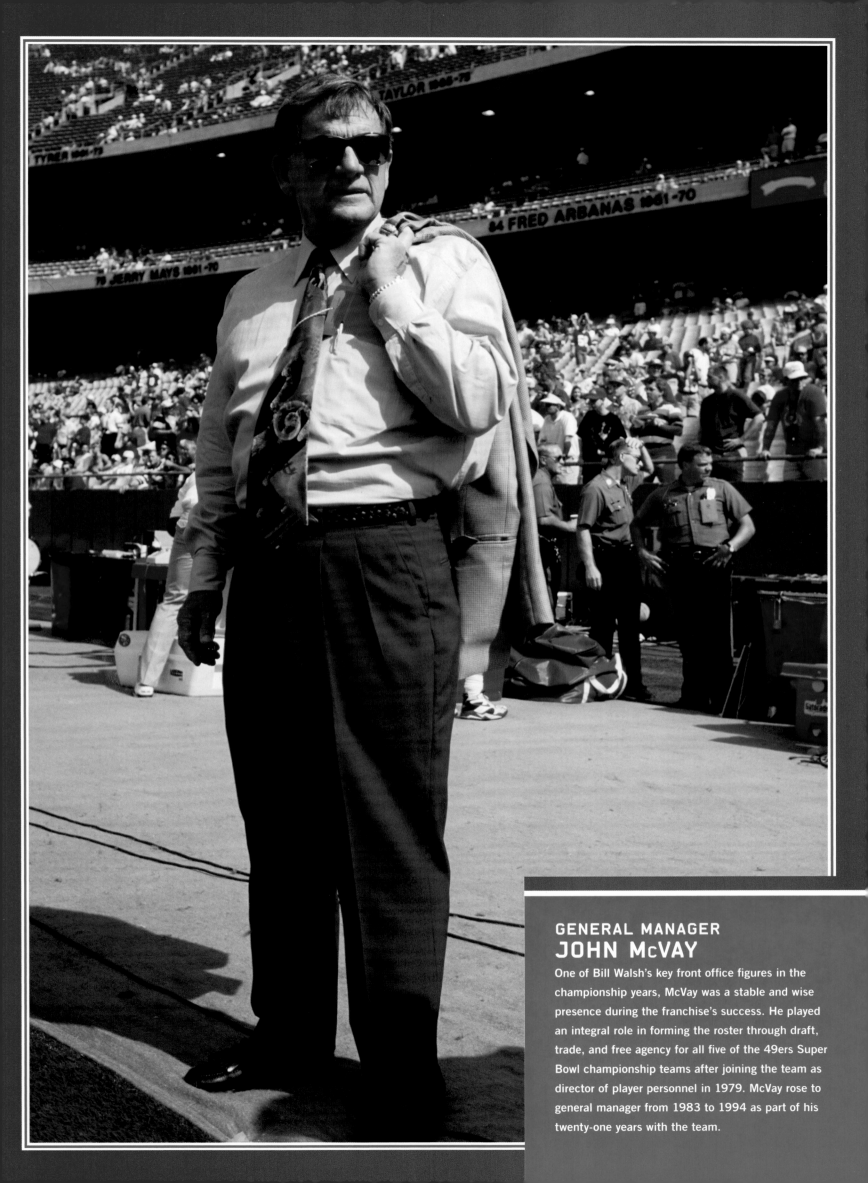

GENERAL MANAGER
JOHN McVAY

One of Bill Walsh's key front office figures in the championship years, McVay was a stable and wise presence during the franchise's success. He played an integral role in forming the roster through draft, trade, and free agency for all five of the 49ers Super Bowl championship teams after joining the team as director of player personnel in 1979. McVay rose to general manager from 1983 to 1994 as part of his twenty-one years with the team.

OPPOSITE: Frank Gore during 2013 playoff win against the Green Bay Packers

TOP: Michael Crabtree scores a touchdown vs. the Baltimore Ravens during Super Bowl XLVII

ABOVE: Vernon Davis celebrates "The Grab," the winning touchdown pass from Alex Smith in the final seconds of the January 14, 2012, playoff vs. the New Orleans Saints

"I always looked at it is as home," Turner said. "Home is much more than a physical space. Home is where you're comfortable. No matter the flaws, it was home. We didn't know any different. I don't know that we ever looked at it as an awful place to play.

"I remember when we'd all transition to football from baseball, and the grass on the infield never had enough time to take," Turner said, then laughed. "I loved it because it meant [Rams running back] Eric Dickerson couldn't get his footing."

As he traveled around on that December evening, Turner was struck. "The stadium served its purpose," he said. "The memories will always be in my heart and will live on. But at the end of the night, I said: 'It's time to go.'"

Steve Young knew it, too. But he also knew that wherever the 49ers went, the lineage would follow. "I can't remember how many people at Candlestick said to me: 'I was in Kezar Stadium,'" Young said. "And how many times I heard: 'I've been in Section 16 at Candlestick.' . . . I think Candlestick bred its own brand of fans."

He took a moment to muse and felt a memory surge. "You're in the locker room," Young said, "and it's dripping from the condensation and from the high tide, and the smell of it is unique, and the fans, you can just hear them . . . 'Beat LA! Beat LA!' . . . And it's just pounding and you're ready to go out there for a Monday Night game. I think the stadium and the fans and San Francisco and the nature of the fog and the wind . . . it's just everything. It was just who we were."

TOP: Jim Harbaugh leads postgame prayer after the 2013 playoff win against the Green Bay Packers

ABOVE: Perrish Cox upends Packers' kick returner during the 2013 playoffs

OPPOSITE: Colin Kaepernick firing up the fans

PAGES 166–167: 49ers fans say farewell to Candlestick Park.

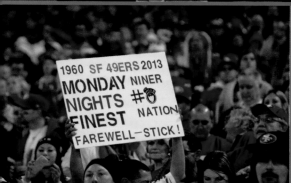

CHAPTER FOUR

INSIDE LEVI'S STADIUM

-10   -20   -30   40

Sixty-eight years after the San Francisco 49ers charged out of the dark, musty tunnel at Kezar Stadium for their first-ever game, and forty-three years after the 49ers charged onto the seam-ridden artificial turf of Candlestick Park for their first game at the 'Stick, the 49ers organization and SCSA cut the ribbons at Levi's Stadium in Santa Clara in the summer of 2014, officially opening a gleaming, $1.2-billion, 1.8-million-square-foot temple of futurism and football.

ABOVE: Levi's Stadium ribbon cutting ceremony

OPPOSITE: Jed York celebrates the ribbon cutting with the construction workers who made Levi's Stadium a reality.

PAGE 172: Levi's Stadium ribbon cutting ceremony

If you want to mail a letter to Levi's Stadium, send it to 4900 Marie P. DeBartolo Way. Then again, given the twenty-first-century technology that dominates the Levi's Stadium experience, you'd be well out of place using snail mail.

Just steps away, at the team's practice facility (known as the SAP Performance Facility) at 4949 Marie P. DeBartolo Way, images of the team's heritage hang in the marble-floored lobby. There is a photo of Levi's Stadium's 2012 groundbreaking, featuring the Yorks and coach Jim Harbaugh in hard hats. There is a photo of Jed York as a small boy, visiting with the late Bill Walsh and his uncle, former owner Eddie DeBartolo Jr., on the sideline of a 49ers road game in Pittsburgh in 1987. And there are black-and-white photos of Tony and Vic Morabito, the 49ers founders from 1946.

If only the Morabitos could see their franchise's new home. They'd probably laugh and say, "Makes Kezar look like the Stone Age."

LEVI'S STADIUM FACTS

- CONCOURSES ARE A SPACIOUS 63 FEET WIDE, MORE THAN THREE TIMES THE BREADTH OF THE CONCOURSES AT CANDLESTICK PARK.

- THE LOWER BOWL OF THE STADIUM SEATS 45,000 FANS.

- THE STADIUM EMPLOYS 45,000 WORKERS ON GAME DAYS, MAKING IT THE FIFTH LARGEST EMPLOYER IN SANTA CLARA.

- 7,788 IS THE TOTAL NUMBER OF MEN AND WOMEN WHO PLAYED A PART IN BUILDING THE STADIUM.

- THE TOTAL LENGTH OF DATA CABLE INSTALLED AT LEVI'S STADIUM IS 400 MILES, ENOUGH TO STRETCH FROM THE STADIUM TO SAN FRANCISCO AND BACK FIVE TIMES.

- 19,200 SQUARE FEET IS THE TOTAL AREA OF THE TWO VIDEO BOARDS BEHIND THE END ZONES.

- THE 515,000-KILOWATT HOURS OF ENERGY THE STADIUM'S SOLAR PANELS PRODUCE IN A SINGLE YEAR COULD POWER THE AVERAGE U.S. HOME FOR 47 YEARS.

- LEVI'S STADIUM HAS 1,135 RESTROOM FIXTURES, 250 MORE THAN CANDLESTICK PARK.

- 9,000 CLUB SEATS ARE AVAILABLE AT LEVI'S STADIUM; THERE WERE ZERO AT CANDLESTICK PARK.

- 180 DIFFERENT MENU ITEMS ARE OFFERED THROUGHOUT THE STADIUM, INCLUDING AT LEAST ONE VEGAN ITEM AT EACH PERMANENT FOOD OUTLET.

- THERE ARE 15 TYPES OF WINE AVAILABLE; EACH COMES FROM CALIFORNIA.

- 85 PERCENT OF THE FOOD SUPPLIERS FOR THE STADIUM ARE LOCATED IN CALIFORNIA.

- THERE ARE 38 ESCALATORS AT LEVI'S STADIUM, WHICH IS 32 MORE THAN AT CANDLESTICK.

- 1,500 IS THE NUMBER OF WI-FI ACCESS POINTS IN LEVI'S STADIUM.

TOP: Fans enjoy the preseason action from the NRG Solar Terrace.

ABOVE: The 49ers SAP Performance Facility is less than a first down from Levi's Stadium.

OPPOSITE TOP: NRG Solar Terrace

OPPOSITE BOTTOM: Field installation

Where to start when describing the vastness of options of Levi's Stadium? Take your pick. You could start with the technology, where you can use your smartphone to figure out which restroom has the shortest line; or the environmentally friendly features, like solar panels powering the place on game day and recycled water feeding the grass; or the team's historical museum, with a re-creation of Bill Walsh's office; or the living roof, with native Bay Area grasses on the only accessible rooftop in the NFL; or the locker room, three and half times bigger than the Candlestick locker room, and so laden with luxury, right down to the walnut-inlaid lockers, it looks like a Four Seasons resort; or the video boards in the north and south end zones, with the one on the south side an enormous 48 feet high and 200 feet wide, with crystal-clear LED and HD pixel layouts, producing replays that look like fine art; or the art collection, featuring culturally diverse works that celebrate both the Bay Area and the 49ers heritage; or the Denise DeBartolo York Educational Center, where schoolchildren from kindergarten through eighth grade will apply the lessons of Levi's Stadium—environmental engineering, irrigation techniques, the physics of a Colin Kaepernick spiral—on 55-inch touchscreen desks; or the restaurants, designed by James Beard Award–winning chef Michael Mina, who will cook on game days; or the clubs and suites, where some fans can high-five players as they make their way from the locker room to the playing field; or the playing field itself, installed in April 2014 in 42-inch strips, atop a pre-installed drainage system, to much acclaim.

ARCHITECT OF THE

$$E = MC^2$$

EXECUTION EQUALS MAKING CATCHES TWO WIN !

B.W. COACH© GENIUS - PROFESSOR   THE CATCH ™.

PASSION + COMMITMENT × DEDICATION
– ADVERSITY (CARRY THE FANS) = A DYNASTY ™.

CREATIVITY IS THE $\sqrt{}$ OF A CHAMPION©

WEST COAST OFFENSE

Architect of the West Coast Offense,
mixed media, by Milton Bowens

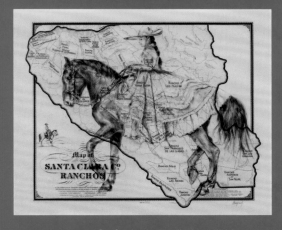

TOP: *The Catch*, mixed media, by Liz Walsh

ABOVE: *Charreria Girl on Horse*, charcoal on paper, by Lynn Hanson

LEVI'S® STADIUM
ART COLLECTION

THE ART COLLECTION AT LEVI'S STADIUM

Perhaps one of the most compelling elements of Levi's Stadium is the fact that it is home to a truly distinctive art collection commissioned specifically for the stadium.

"We were looking for innovative ways to enhance the gameday experience for our fans. We felt an art collection that highlights all that is special about the Bay Area and its football team was a unique way to achieve that goal," said 49ers vice president of marketing Ali Towle.

After conducting a public call for artists, the 49ers, in partnership with Sports and the Arts, who served as curators for the collection, selected twenty-three artists to contribute. The roster of artists includes local talent as well as established veterans. Several of the local artists are exhibiting their works for the first time.

The results—more than 200 pieces of original artwork ranging from larger-than-life oil and watercolor paintings to smaller pen, ink, and charcoal sketches and from bronze sculptures to found-object art. The collection also includes more than 500 photographs from the archives of the 49ers and their esteemed group of team photographers and media partners.

"A majority of the collection features local artists who are actual 'Certified Faithful' fans," said Towle. "This unique opportunity allowed them to showcase what California and the 49ers legendary history means to them, making the collection even more eclectic."

No other multiuse stadium contains the quantity and scope of original artwork that the Levi's Stadium collection has procured. The 49ers are thrilled to present a collection that enhances the building, while engaging everyone from the casual football fan to the art aficionado.

THESE PAGES: Details of the plush 49ers locker room

The 49ers will charge onto the field from an entryway so far different from the Kezar days it nearly defies comparison. The Kezar tunnel, remember, came from a high school–style locker room and was so dim and foreboding that Y. A. Tittle likened it to a Roman Colosseum tunnel leading to the lions. The path players tread at Levi's Stadium is rather different.

From a locker room with cavernous walnut-paneled lockers—where a lounge features five HDTVs, where a physio room features a gigantic cold tub, hot tub, and treadmill pool—the team crosses a carpeted path through the BNY Mellon Club, where patrons pay $80,000 to be a member. From there, the Levi's Stadium turf awaits, just outside the club's glass doors.

Outside and nearby the team's locker room, players' significant others and close family and children can be entertained by the built-in day care Family Room while their loved one in football gear is introduced elaborately on the HD Sony and Daktronics video board with specially-produced film pieces. Those video boards, 19,200 square feet of them, can access up to a maximum of thirty-two HD cameras. Candlestick Park, you may recall, had no fascia video boards, and somewhere around 18,000 fewer square feet of presentation.

The locker room—a phrase that conjures a den of smelly sweat—hardly conveys the deluxe décor of Levi's Stadium changing quarters, which feature so many comforts because the team will also use it during the season on practice days, not just on game days.

ABOVE AND OPPOSITE: 49ers pass through the BNY Mellon Club as they make their way to the field.

PAGES 184–185: View of the field from the Verizon Press Level.

One catch is, it's on the opposite side of the stadium from the Verizon Press Level, where 49ers coaches call the game. At halftime, 49ers coaches need to get from their box to the locker room as soon as possible. At Candlestick, this journey was a logistical maze that required an often-unrewarded faith that the elevator would be in operating order, followed by a fight against the crowd, like salmon swimming upstream, and a sprint across the field to the locker room. Essentially, haste was impossible. At Levi's Stadium, however, seven elevators—of twenty-five stadium-wide, to

go along with thirty-six escalators—are used from the service corridor to the Verizon Press Level. Coaches now only need a golf cart ride through a service corridor—no need to swim upstream against a gaggle of fans in Kaepernick jerseys going to get their navy bean and kale curry or their Peking duck bao. Though the press box is on the other side of the stadium, the locker room is a minute away.

All the while, well outside the locker room and service corridor, fans are living in a different world than they ever imagined.

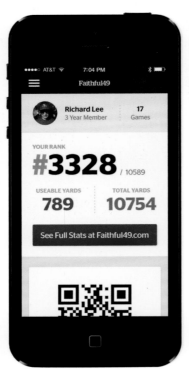

With stadium-wide Wi-Fi, Levi's Stadium has forever changed the in-game experience for fans. This is the challenge of live entertainment in the twenty-first century: How to compete with the in-home experience? According to the 49ers chief operating officer Al Guido, the answer is "convenience."

To make fans feel like their experience at Levi's Stadium is even more convenient and expansive than their in-home experience, Bluetooth beacons identify your smartphone on your Levi's Stadium app, with Wi-Fi coming from every direction—even from under your seat.

This allows fans, from their seats, to study the concessions menus, which range from traditional, "old-school" hot dogs and burgers to a more eclectic Bay Area–flavored blend of fresh-and-organic, ethnically diverse dishes, like a golden beet salad, an oyster pan roast, or a BBQ jackfruit sandwich. Then, you can choose between "express pickup"—while viewing the nearest stand and quickest line—or in-seat delivery, the better to not miss any 49ers action.

Wondering when that beer you ordered will be coming? Wait times are provided based on a real-time simulation engine on your smartphone. The goal is not to miss 49ers football while waiting in an agonizing line. "In-seat delivery means you don't have to miss Kap's next touchdown pass," president Paraag Marathe said.

Ordering food and drink with your phone at your seat is only the start of Levi's Stadium's technological offerings. Cognizant of the allure of HDTV in your living room, Levi's Stadium is equipped with multiple cameras with feeds accessible on your phone. Slow-motion, HD replays are available within seconds if you want to call up the "Kap Cam" or the "Vernon Cam" or whatever camera replay suits your desire. Cameras may even follow a player into the locker room. Point is, at Levi's Stadium, you can watch it. At home, you can't.

"We want to provide fans with content they can't get at home," Guido said. "To enhance the experience, but still keep the tradition of a 49ers game."

THESE PAGES: The Stadium App delivers a number of revolutionary, stadium experience–enhancing features, including concessions ordering and game replay.

Transfer Ticket >

YOUR SEAT

On the Main Concourse

Make your way to the Main Concourse and walk towards row 200. Lorem ipsum dolor sit amet, conse ctetur adip iscing elit.

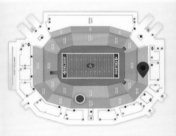

Get Directions >

CLUB ACCESS

YAHOO! Fantasy Football Lounge	🚶 4 min	>
Levi's VIP Lounge	🚶 8 min	>
49ers Faithful Lounge	🚶 12 min	>

AT&T 7:04 PM

< My Order $50.04

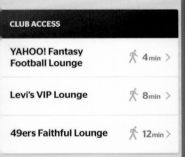

Steamed Buns

14
SF

2nd & 7
@ SEA 37 | 11:50 Q2

0
SEA

Game Replay

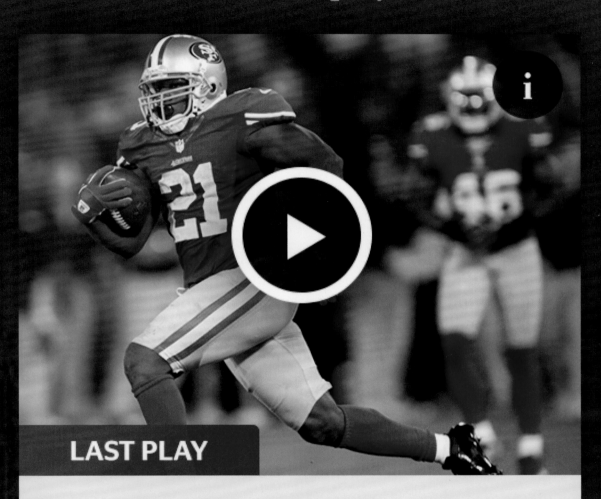

LAST PLAY

Run 17 Yds
1st & 10 @ Seattle 27

Frank Gore runs right for a gain of 17 yards and a 49ers 1st down.

"On and off the field, talent alone will not lead to success. The game changer for promising future leaders is to provide a stimulating environment where their natural talent and drive will be fed by motivating mentors, meaningful activities, and academic enrichment. The 49ers STEM Leadership Institute's vision is to be a leader in STEM education, preparing and inspiring talented learners to meet the challenges of the global society through innovation, collaboration, and creative problem solving."

—JOHN YORK, CO-CHAIRMAN OF THE SAN FRANCISCO 49ERS

Funded by the 49ers Foundation, Chevron and other collaborative partners, through a six-year program, the 49ers STEM Leadership Institute's Chevron STEMZONE will take academically talented students and provide tools for them to be outstanding STEM leaders. The Institute will prepare them to engage in scientific research, participate in impactful community-changing projects, or become entrepreneurs— putting them on the path to enroll in a top-tier university with a STEM major. Housed at Cabrillo Middle School in Santa Clara, each year, the Institute will recruit rising seventh grade students from Santa Clara Unified School District who show academic promise or who are highly motivated to succeed.

> "We stepped back and said: How can we really do something that nobody's doing in pro sports?"

TOP: Students engage in an interactive lesson at the Denise DeBartolo York Educational Center.

ABOVE: Denise DeBartolo York engages with a student at the Denise DeBartolo York Educational Center.

Technology is something that is taught at the Denise DeBartolo York Educational Center, which is located inside the 49ers Museum presented by Sony and is perhaps the stadium feature that is nearest and dearest to the York family. Museum director Jesse Lovejoy called it the "heart and soul of the museum," and it fulfills the Yorks' desire to educate local school children in STEM—science, technology, engineering, and math—to better compete in our twenty-first-century economy.

More than twenty thousand local schoolchildren a year will be bused, free of charge, to Levi's Stadium, given a tour of the stadium and the museum, and then brought to the Educational Center for a hands-on STEM lesson. The idea is to use football as a platform to teach, hoping that "moments of inspiration," as the Yorks put it, can translate into learning.

For example, the tour of the solar panels that serve the stadium can lead to a lesson in alternative energy, providing some real-world meaning to the phrase "net neutral on the grid." Or a review of the field and explanation of how it's irrigated can lead to a discussion of environmental engineering. Or the study of that Kaepernick spiral could lead to a lesson in physics—*in the absence of gravity, kids, that perfect spiral would mean Michael Crabtree would be going deep, to the rings of Saturn even, for a catch.* And on and on. The key is removing all barriers for kids to learn.

"Maybe this will get them excited about something they never associated with football before," said Lovejoy. "We stepped back and said: How can we really do something that nobody's doing in pro sports? This is legit. This isn't some scavenger hunt. This isn't a passing nod to education. This is a standards-aligned, high-quality experience."

THESE PAGES: The 49ers Museum presented by Sony offers 20,000 square feet of interactive content and treasures from the storied past of the 49ers, including the ball and piece of turf from the spot where Dwight Clark made "The Catch."

For children on their way to the Denise DeBartolo York Educational Center, the 20,000-square-foot museum will surely get the juices flowing, but the museum isn't just for kids. It's open to the public, year-round, and it gives the five-time Super Bowl champions their full historical due. According to Peter Sollogub of the museum design team C7A, "the museum celebrates the aura and mystique of the 49ers. It's as simple as that, and it led us to places in the heart."

To control the flow of the crowd, and to set the right tone for the visit, a museum tour begins with a stop in the ninety-person theater, which presents an 18-minute film on the team history. Energized by images of "The Catch," Kezar, and Ronnie Lott, visitors then move into the main museum space, a wavelike structure that simulates the flow of a spiral pass, perhaps one thrown by Joe Montana, Steve Young, John Brodie, or Y. A. Tittle. C7A's design goal was to make the space feel liquid and fluid, like the West Coast offense, taking the visitor on an exciting journey into the 49ers decorated past.

Team artifacts hang inside the infinite spiral, giving a sense of movement, and the museum includes a re-creation of a place where one of football's most legendary dynasties began: Bill Walsh's office, which is filled with artifacts from Walsh's personal collection donated by his son, Craig Walsh. The reverential should take a moment to ponder the draft picks and play calls that sprung from that very desk.

The patch of grass where Dwight Clark landed after "The Catch" . . . all five touchdown balls from Ricky Watters's NFL-record five-TD game in a January 1994 playoff win versus the New York Giants . . . a re-created locker from Kezar Stadium: All of it was carefully planned and researched by the team to provide an amazing educational experience.

The Edward DeBartolo, Sr., 49ers Hall of Fame has grown along with the team's own presence in the Pro Football Hall of Fame in Canton, Ohio.

THE BALL. THE SPOT. THE CATCH.

On January 10, 1982, Joe Montana made
Sprint Right Option famous when he threw this
ball toward the back of the end zone with 58
seconds remaining in the 1981 NFC Championship
Game. Dwight Clark leaped, caught the ball with his
fingertips and landed on this spot in Candlestick
Park's north end zone, forever cementing
"The Catch" in professional football history as the
symbolic beginning of the 49ers era of dominance
and as one of the greatest plays of all time.

This ball is on loan to the 49ers Museum
thanks to the generosity of William F. McDonagh, Jr.

MUSEUM
PRESENTED BY SONY

THESE PAGES: One of the keynotes of the 49ers Museum presented by Sony is the live-size statues of key 49ers personalities that capture iconic moments from 49er history, including Dwight Clark making "The Catch" (above), and the Million Dollar Backfield (bottom right).

PAGES 194–195: Details from the 49ers Museum

There are no static bronze busts in the Levi's Stadium museum, however. Instead, StudioEIS has turned every 49ers legend inducted into the team Hall of Fame—from Leo Nomellini and Bob St. Clair to Jimmy Johnson, from Dave Wilcox to Joe Montana and Jerry Rice and Steve Young—into a life-size statue, in full stride, clad in the uniform of their era. Gordy Soltau, from the Kezar years, is kicking a football. Lott sneers, game-face on, as you leave the theater and enter the museum. They may have played decades apart, but the museum puts them in the same room at the peak of their careers—a 49ers Dream Team for the ages.

Finally, the museum visit ends in the gallery of championships, where the five Super Bowl trophies are displayed uncovered, open to the air, not encased yet not touchable, producing what Peter Sollogub describes as a "calming and elegant" tribute.

How much 49ers history was there to summarize? Put it this way: The original plans called for 5,000 square feet of museum space. They needed, and used, every inch of 20,000.

After all that, or even before all that, fans need a place to sit, gather, and eat. Ideally, they'd want to do so in a style familiar and comfortable for the Northern California palate. Enter celebrity chef Michael Mina, the Michelin-starred, Bay Area–based gastronome who happens to be a huge 49ers fan and a twenty-two-year season-ticket holder as well.

Hence, Michael Mina's Bourbon Steak & Pub at Levi's Stadium, which is open year-round, and Michael Mina's Tailgate, right next door, where the sweet TVs, sound system, and fare will make it "the neighborhood's best sports bar," in the words of one designer.

Since all of Levi's Stadium aims to redefine the in-stadium fan experience, Mina didn't want to be left out. Bourbon Steak & Pub features two pieces of kitchen theater not to be missed: a two-story rotisserie that is 13 feet long, 13 feet tall, and 7 feet wide and contains a "ferris wheel of rotating food," according to food designer Ken Schwartz. The rotisserie can hold an entire ox, some 800 pounds, on its skewer. But that's not all.

Mina also wants to cook seafood, and he wants to cook seafood for 49ers fans in style. So, SSA (Systems Services of America) designed a "seafood station" of the highest order, with three giant boiling pots, each 4 feet in diameter, to boil shrimp, crab, and lobster. The pots can hold 144 gallons of water and, when full, weigh up to 1,400 pounds.

Architects and designers were told at the outset of the project that Levi's Stadium would need to emphasize the food and wine of the region. Michael Mina is making sure this vision comes to fruition.

Architects and designers were told at the outset of the project that Levi's Stadium would need to emphasize the food and wine of the region. Michael Mina is making sure this vision comes to fruition.

PAGES 196–197: Another showcase of the 49ers Museum presented by Sony is the reproduction of Bill Walsh's office.

THESE PAGES: Michael Mina's Bourbon Steak & Pub

PAGES 200–201: Michael Mina's Tailgate

In the end, Levi's Stadium offers a great all around experience. Pedestrian flow is fluid, a far cry from the cramped Candlestick days. The sound system, often muted by wind gusts and acoustic trouble at Candlestick, is vastly improved, so much so that VP of stadium operations Jim Mercurio, a veteran of the Candlestick years, joked before the ribbon cutting, "Hopefully, fans will actually be able to hear the announcements."

Guido says he can't believe he went from knocking on doors for votes in 2010 to giving tours of Levi's Stadium in the summer of 2014, wowing season-ticket holders. He watches their reactions, and he sees them shocked at Levi's Stadium amenities.

"It's one thing to see a chart or rendering of the place," 49ers chief operating officer Al Guido said. "It's another to go out there. And then you hear, 'This is amazing!' I mean, at Candlestick, every suite faced home plate for baseball. Now they look at the concourse width . . . the sightlines. . . .

"I hear them say: It's so big, and so intimate, and those beautiful video boards. I couldn't ever see a replay at Candlestick." Guido added, "A lot of people never thought this would happen. I lived all the stories about people upset about pricing, about the move, people not understanding leaving five Super Bowl trophies behind at Candlestick. That's a lot to ask people to change from. I'm most proud of the fans and their commitment to be willing to go on this ride with us."

OPPOSITE: Immaculate weather provided a fine backdrop for the 2014 49ers preseason victory over the San Diego Chargers.

Linebacker Michael Wilhoite greets fans (ABOVE),
and the 49ers get fired up for an exciting future at
Levi's Stadium (RIGHT).

As a Candlestick alum, Jim Mercurio can provide the best vantage of them all. He is wowed by the number of restrooms, which he called "grandiose and accommodating." He says Levi's Stadium concession stands are more open and free, with true options. He notes the focus on original and cool food items. "And how about that paperless ticket entry," he said, remembering the long lines to enter the stadium at Candlestick.

"It's an attractive building," he said. "It has an airy feel to it. You feel free." And the sightlines, he said, "are incredible." No longer will TV capture a wedge of empty seats behind Candlestick's rollout bleachers, over near the old Berkeley Farms Junior 49er Minor Club section in the southeast end zone.

For the ultimate vantage, though, head to the rooftop. There, the native grasses sway in the South Bay breeze. You look down and see 100 yards of football field, the same measurements at Kezar and at Candlestick, and yet so different. The view is breathtaking. Weddings were already booked there before the stadium opened.

From that rooftop, you can see a lot: the rolling hills of the East Bay, the skyline of San Jose, the horizon leading to the Santa Cruz Mountains. Look north and you see the happy memories of the 49ers past, on a clear day, all the way to the San Francisco skyline. Look down on the field and you see the vibrant images of the 49ers now.

On a cloudless and still 78-degree South Bay early evening, 49ers kicker Phil Dawson kicked off a new era in the history of the Bay Area's oldest original pro sports franchise.

PAGES 208-209: Pat Monahan of Train sings the "Star-Spangled Banner" in front of a sold-out crowd to help christen Levi's Stadium on opening day

ABOVE: Light rail helped usher in a portion of the 70,799 fans who attended opening day

OPPOSITE AND PAGES 214-215: Fans entering Levi's Stadium through Intel Gate A can hit the team store and grab a drink at the Kezar Sports Bar, or any number of other concession stands, before strolling the main concourse to their seats

PAGES 212-213: The outward façade of the suite tower boldly proclaims the moment many 49ers fans have been anticipating for years: the inaugural season at Levi's Stadium

PAGES 216-217: Fans fired up for opening day

It was 5:30 p.m. on September 14, 2014, short-sleeve weather, and time for a vision and a dream to become reality. Levi's Stadium was hosting real, live NFL football. 49ers football. NBC's "Sunday Night Football" team was there to broadcast it, and 20 million viewers soaked it in. The 49ers and Chicago Bears had played each other before, but never in a 21st-century building, in the heart of Silicon Valley, with amenities the fans at the September 1946 game at Kezar Stadium never could have dreamed of.

Everywhere you looked, concepts became reality. The SAP Tower, painted bone white, shimmered as the dipping sun reflected off it. As evening encroached, and lights illuminated the tower, the red "Levi's" batwing beamed off the snow-colored architecture, a striking sight. Tuxedo-clad ushers reported the "Express Pickup" for fans using the Stadium App, and food and beverages moved swimmingly. Michael Mina's Bourbon Steak & Pub fed fans with world-class food, while Michael Mina's Tailgate broadcasted all the early NFL games. Fans toured the 49ers Museum presented by Sony. They absorbed the emotionally powerful eighteen-minute historical film, surveyed the life-size statues of the Hall-of-Famers, and were touched by memorabilia as dramatic as the five Super Bowl trophies, and as evocative as an old street sign pointing the way to Candlestick Park, with a baseball player and football player indicating the old stadium's dual tenants. Inside Levi's Stadium, the spectacular video boards in the north and south end zones dazzled 70,799 fans, most with red 49ers jerseys declaring their loyalties. Eye-popping high definition replays and complete statistical progress of the game flew by on the impressive screens.

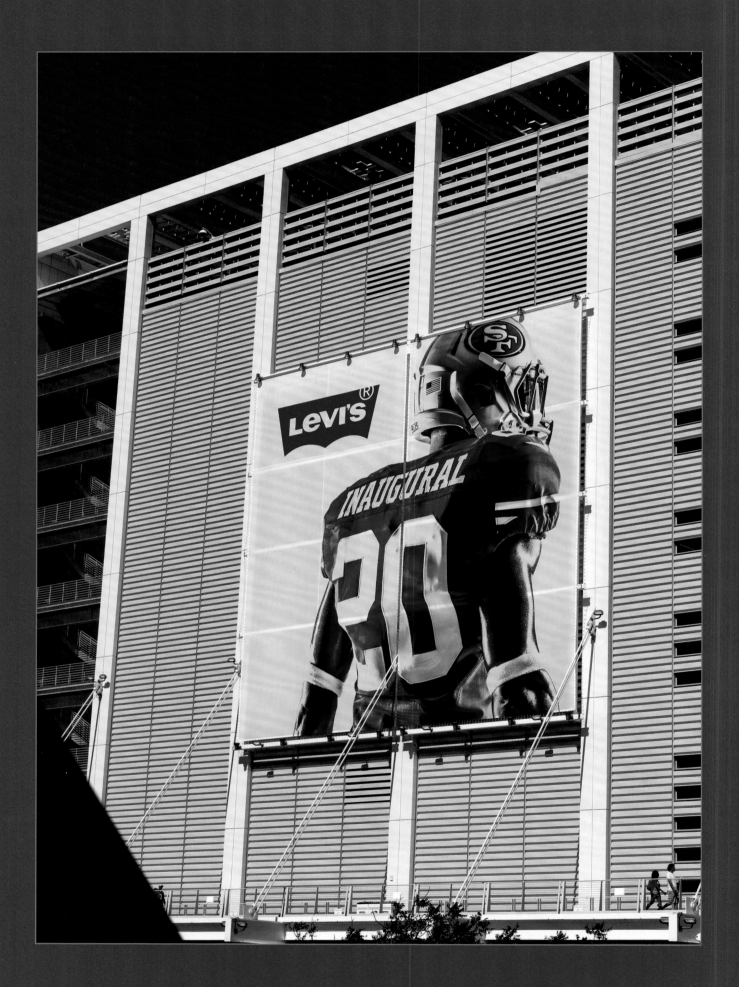

OPPOSITE TOP: Michael Mina's Tailgate saw a host of fans enjoying an upscale, all-inclusive, game-themed menu as well as the "early game" action from around the country on the many HDTVs

ABOVE: The 49ers Flagship Team Store at Levi's Stadium features more than 13,000 square feet of merchandise, including specialty shops for Levi's, Nike, New Era, and Mitchell & Ness

OPPOSITE BOTTOM: Chef Michael Mina

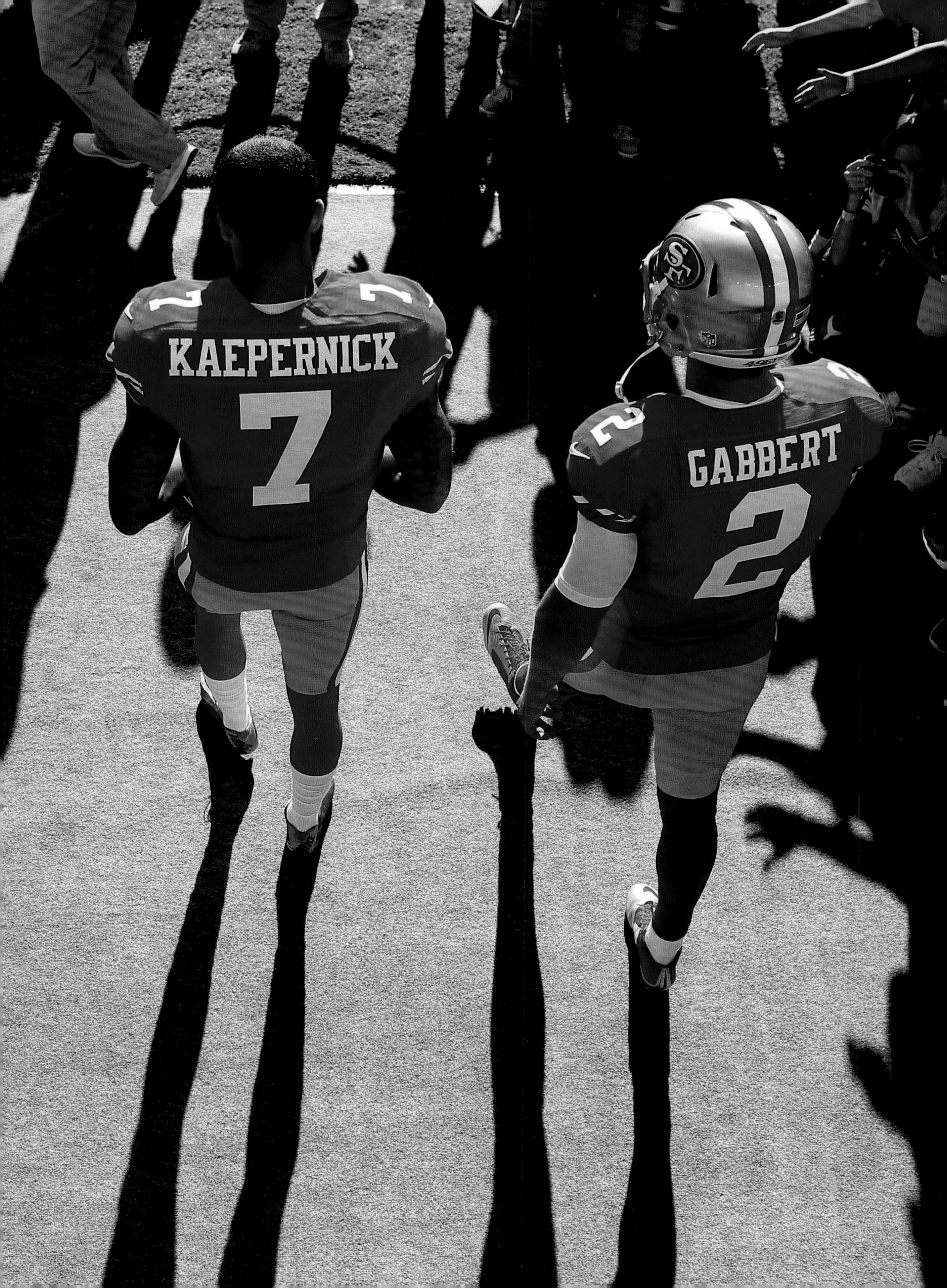
KAEPERNICK
7
GABBERT
2

PAGE 220: Colin Kaepernick and Blaine Gabbert emerge onto the field from the BNY Mellon Club for their pre-game warm-up

PAGE 221, TOP: Field view of Levi's Stadium with Patrick Willis on the sideline during warm-up

PAGE 221, BOTTOM: The 49ers emerge from the BNY Mellon Club for their pre-game warm-up

PAGES 222–223: 49ers get fired up after opening day warm-up

ABOVE: The 49ers flag bearers and Sourdough Sam charge out on the field in advance of the team to announce the 49ers

OPPOSITE: Left to right: Vance McDonald, Perrish Cox, and Nick Moody charge onto the field on opening day

Before the video boards, 200 feet wide, beamed the striking images of rookie Aaron Lynch blocking the first punt in Levi's Stadium, snuffing Bears punter Pat O'Donnell's attempt to boot the ball and giving the 49ers the ball on Chicago's 8-yard line, before the 48-foot-tall video boards showed replay after replay of the first NFL touchdown in Levi's Stadium history—an ensuing 3-yard first quarter pass from Colin Kaepernick to Michael Crabtree—the video boards provided an emotional, resonant welcome.

At 5:01 p.m., a six-minute film began with the voice of Oscar-nominated actor Jeremy Renner, an avowed 49ers fanatic, speaking over images of 49ers football, past and present. As Renner spoke, and as an NFL Films–styled orchestra played its martial strains, the screens flashed the sights of Kezar Stadium, the Million Dollar Backfield, early 1970s 49ers like Hall-of-Famer Jimmy Johnson, fans exulting at Candlestick, and the professorial presence of Bill Walsh emerging from a locker room. The at-times grainy film lent the video an artistic sheen.

"They know who we are," Renner said. "There are millions of us. They don't call us fans or bandwagoners. They definitely don't call us a 'Nation.' They know our name. They know what we're about." Renner appeared on screen in jeans, a leather jacket, and a vintage 49ers shirt. He stared into the camera. "We're the 49ers Faithful," he continued, "and we've been doing this for years."

What ensued was an artistic free form of sights and sounds, from Steve Young to the Morabito Brothers, from Leo "The Lion" Nomellini to Joe Montana, from Eddie DeBartolo Jr. to Jed York, from Gordy Soltau to Jim Harbaugh. If a 49ers fan didn't get coated in goose flesh, he or she wasn't watching.

> "There are millions of us. They don't call us fans or bandwagoners. They definitely don't call us a 'Nation.' They know our name. They know what we're about. . . . We're the 49ers Faithful, and we've been doing this for years."

PAGES 226–227: Chicago Bears punter Pat O'Donnell is blocked by Aaron Lynch

OPPOSITE: Michael Crabtree scores the first regular season touchdown at Levi's Stadium

ABOVE: A sea of red and gold proclaims Levi's Stadium is 49ers territory

After the film, and fireworks, and before kickoff, there was the matter of opening the game with the "Star-Spangled Banner." Bay Area recording artist Pat Monahan of Train stood at midfield to sing it, on a riser, above an American flag that blanketed the entire field. The offense was introduced, with each player taking the field to a snazzy video presentation. Introduced last, to the delight of the Faithful, was Frank Gore, the longest-tenured 49er on the 2014 team. Gore would score a touchdown, too. His 8-yard scamper into the north end zone made it 49ers 17, Bears 0 in the second quarter, and all seemed right in the world.

ABOVE: 49ers offensive line poised pre-snap

OPPOSITE: Frank Gore powers his way to the end zone for the second-ever regular season touchdown at Levi's Stadium

PAGES 232–233: Left to right: 49ers Ian Williams, Patrick Willis, and Perrish Cox

Even after a rousing halftime performance by recording artist Snoop Dogg, and even after a 17-7 49ers halftime lead extended to 20-7 on a third quarter field goal by Dawson, the Bears, behind big-armed quarterback Jay Cutler, struck late. The big party didn't have a happy ending: Bears 28, 49ers 20.

If there were any consolation, it's that the 49ers had traveled this road before. Kezar Stadium's first game, on Sept, 8, 1946, went to the New York Yankees of the All-American Football Conference, 21-7 over the 49ers, despite a memorable touchdown pass from Frankie Albert to Len Eshmont. And the 49ers first game at Candlestick Park, on October 10, 1971, saw the 49ers stumble late, allowing 10 unanswered fourth-quarter points to the Los Angeles Rams in a 20-13 Rams victory. So, it's happened before. The organization preferred, instead, to find strength in the words from Renner's powerful narration, reminding them of their past, and pointing toward their future, understanding that the one constant, besides the uniforms and logos and footballs, are the fans.

"This won't be a stadium for 'The Wave' or for fair-weather fans who just bought their jerseys last week," Renner said before the first game in Levi's Stadium history. "No. This is our new home. It's where the faith never ends. It's where history will be remembered and celebrated. This will be the hallowed place where the ghosts of the past connect with the united heartbeat of everyone in these seats. . . . Look around. Our heroes are everywhere. They're next to you. They're on the field. They're looking down on us. But as important as the greatest names to grace this team have been, it is the Faithful that makes the 49ers what they are."

Levi's Stadium was officially open, and the 49ers were playing football. At long last.

THESE PAGES: Snoop Dogg put on a rousing halftime performance, honoring the "West Coast Offense" popularized by Bill Walsh with some West Coast hip-hop.

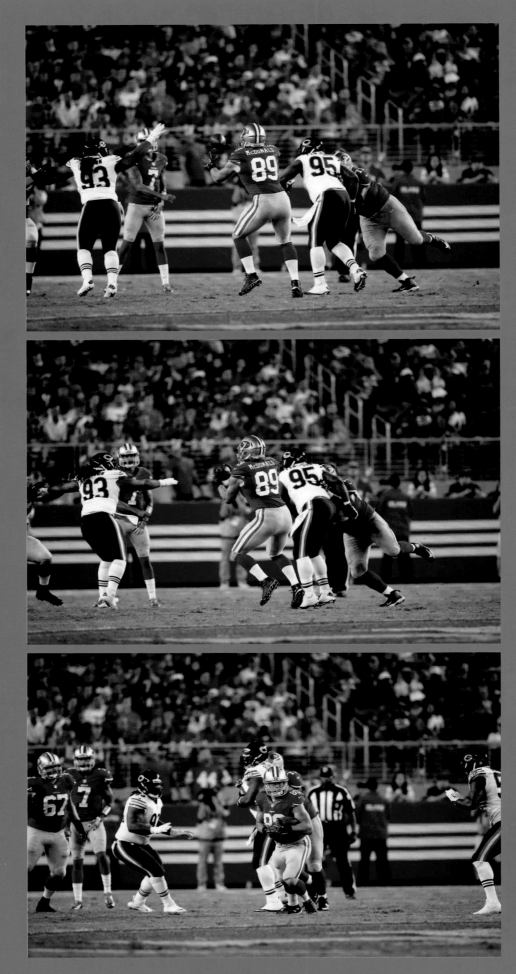

ABOVE: Kaepernick links up with Vance McDonald for a short gain

OPPOSITE: Alex Boone (left) and Daniel Kilgore (right) give
Kaepernick some much-needed pass protection

PAGES 238–239: Justin Smith fired up after sacking Bears' quarterback Jay Cutler during the first quarter of the Levi's Stadium opener

OPPOSITE: Anquan Boldin

ABOVE: 49ers defensive team making their last stand against the Bears

PAGES 242–243: Colin Kaepernick

ABOVE: Wide-angle views from inside Levi's Stadium at dusk

OPPOSITE: Levi's Stadium lighting up the Santa Clara night,
a beacon for 49ers Faithful across the Bay Area and beyond

49ERS MUSEUM PRESENTED BY SONY

In August 2014 the doors swung open at the 49ers Museum at Levi's Stadium, changing the game for sports museums across the world. A home of innovation, education, and 49ers heritage, the museum is a first-class celebration of the 49ers past, present, and future.

Paying off the vision of the York Family—to create an area where children could be inspired to learn and achieve, and fans could celebrate the team's history and innovatively interact with content—the 49ers Museum is a space that fans around the world will visit to dive further into what it means to be a member of the 49ers Faithful. Once inside the museum, guests will weave their way through an artistically influenced architectural design while enjoying eleven unique galleries and countless elements of interest. A pilgrimage is a must for any fan of the red & gold. Visit **www.Levisstadium.com/Museum** to learn more.

ACKNOWLEDGMENTS

Insight Editions would like to thank Jerry Rice and Jed York for their contributions to this project, and a big thanks to Brian Murphy for his tireless efforts and great story telling. We would also like to thank everyone at the 49ers, as a Bay Area publisher it has been an honor working with this legendary franchise. A special thanks to Jackie Brans for her day-to-day efforts, Morrie Eisenberg, Jesse Lovejoy, and Beth Atlas.

Additionally we would like to thank the photographers involved: Terrell Lloyd for his incredible football photography and for getting us the details we needed to show off Levi's Stadium; the late Frank Rippon whose images from the Kezar era are true treasures, as well as Frank's son, Steve Rippon; and Michael Zagaris—his images of the 49ers glory years are peerless and his insight priceless.

The 49ers would like to thank Denise DeBartolo York, Dr. John York, Jed York, Trent Baalke, Paraag Marathe, Al Guido, Cipora Herman, Ethan Casson, Larry MacNeil, Patty Inglis, Hannah Gordon, Keena Turner, Terrell Lloyd, Morrie Eisenberg, Ali Towle, Mike Chasanoff, Dan Beckler, Bob Lange, Roger Hacker, Bob Sargent, Rob Alberino, Brent Schoeb, Joanne Pasternack, Jesse Lovejoy, Beth Atlas, Martin Manville, Daniel Webster-Clark, and Jackie Brans.

And a special thank you to our corporate partners: Levi's®, Anheuser-Busch, BNY Mellon, Brocade, Chevron, Citrix, Cumulus, Dignity Health, Esurance, Intel, KPIX, NRG, Optum, Pepsi, Safeway, SAP, Sony, SunPower, Tickemaster, Toyota, United Airlines, U.S. Bank, Verizon, Violin Memory, Visa, Xfinity, and Yahoo!

PHOTO CREDITS